M

LAND OF

Milk

— AND —

Honey

THE STORY OF TRADITIONAL

IRISH FOOD & DRINK

BRÍD MAHON

with an introduction by
KATHLEEN WATKINS

POOLBEG

TO MARIE FOR HER ENCOURAGEMENT AND KATHLEEN
FOR HER HELP

First published 1991 by
Poolbeg Press Ltd
Knocksedan House,
Swords, Co Dublin, Ireland

© Bríd Mahon, 1991
© Introduction and linking passages to recipes, Kathleen Watkins, 1991

The moral right of the author has been asserted.

ISBN 1 85371 142 X

Cover design and chapter illustration by Pomphrey Associates
Cover photograph courtesy of Bord Fáilte
Set by Richard Parfrey in Palatino 10/13
Printed by The Guernsey Press Company Ltd,
Vale, Guernsey, Channel Islands

Contents

Acknowledgements

The author wishes to thank her colleagues on the staff of the Department of Irish Folklore, University College, Dublin: in particular Professor Bo Almquist for his permission to use the manuscript material of the Archives and for directing her to references in the Icelandic sagas, and to Professor Séamas Ó Catháin who was unfailingly generous with his time and knowledge. She also wishes to thank her former colleagues in the Irish Folklore Commission: Dr Seán Ó Súilleabháin, Dr Kevin Danaher, the folklore collectors in the field, and the tradition-bearers who gave unstintingly of their knowledge. She remembers with affection and gratitude the late Dr Séamus Ó Duilearga, Honorary Director of the Irish Folklore Commission, without whose inspiration and dedication to the task of preserving the heritage of the Irish people the priceless material to be found in the manuscripts would have been lost for ever.

Amongst her colleagues and friends in University College she wishes to record her thanks to the late Dr Kevin O'Nolan, Professor Proinsias Ní Chatháin, Professor Tomás de Bhaldraithe, Professor Proinsias Mac Cana and Professor Michael Herity for their help and advice.

And finally she wishes to express her appreciation of the encouragement and help given her by the late Dr Anthony Lucas, former Director of the National Museum of Ireland, who first suggested that she embark on this task.

Introduction

BY

KATHLEEN WATKINS

Over the last five years it has been my very great pleasure to travel with the *Faces and Places* TV crews all over this beautiful country of ours. People from all walks of life have welcomed us into their homes and their places of work and we have had a most wonderful experience, one which we will never forget.

What we have noticed is that people in Ireland in the Nineties are eating different kinds of foods. That is true not only of homes and small restaurants, but of our top class restaurants where we have our own chefs who have trained here in Shannon Training School and at Cathal Brugha Street and indeed many of them at different training schools in Switzerland. We have a standard of cuisine now that is as good as and in some cases better than in French restaurants or some of the top restaurants you'll find in any other country.

I think what we have above all and what we should appreciate— and I really do think that many people *do* appreciate it—is the best food from the source. We have Irish lamb and beef, we have fish from the sea, fresh vegetables and good dairy produce. For example, in the farm attached to Darina Allen's famous cookery school at Ballymaloe and at her mother-in-law's wonderful country house they have free-range hens. There is a flavour that is second to none and you can see the colour in the beautiful egg mayonnaises and in sponge cakes. When you taste these foods you realise that it would be a shame if we were ever to lose them in the Nineties. We're probably going to have to pay a little more for the very best food, fresh from the source, but it will be worth it.

I have known Bríd Mahon as a folklorist for many years and have many of her books in my house. I'm delighted for Brid that this book is being published and I know she is very pleased about it herself. She has worked long and hard on the book but what I love about it is that it is written very simply and it is the kind of book that anybody of any age would enjoy reading. I wish her every success with it.

SIXTEENTH-CENTURY WOODCUT DEPICTING AN IRISH CHIEFTAIN
BEING ENTERTAINED BY POET AND HARPER.

(From Derricke's *The Image of Ireland*)

1

The Way We Were

They are shadowy, nomadic figures, the Sandelian and Larnian folk who were our first ancestors. On the plains and in the great forests they hunted and trapped the red deer and wild pig; they fished the rivers for salmon, trout and eels, snared pigeon, duck, grouse and the capercaillie—a bird of the pine forest which became extinct in the 18th century. They gathered oysters, limpets and periwinkles in the shallows and hazelnuts in the greenwoods. So much we know about them, and little else.

The image changes; the picture grows clearer; the hunters, fishers and food-gatherers have vanished into the dim past to be replaced by the first farmers, who arrived on our shores around six thousand years ago. They crossed the sea in their light curach-type boats, carrying their bags of seed corn and their farming implements. For them it was a voyage of discovery. They were not disappointed in what they found: a green island with mighty woods of pine and elm, oak and hazel, rivers teeming with fish, bushes laden with fruit, a delightful climate, warm enough to ensure that there would be twelve months' growth of grass, fodder for their animals. In those far-off days Ireland had a climate more equable than today.

These Neolithic farmers were not only experienced in crop cultivation and animal husbandry but also in the sister crafts of spinning, weaving and pottery-making. With their polished stone axe-heads they set about clearing shrubs and trees and, as they did so, the elms they had been struggling so hard to overcome died away and a great fertile stretch of land opened up before them. They had found their Hy Brasil, their Plain of Honey. Henceforth this would be their home. They built houses, cultivated farms, grew wheat and barley, increased their herds of cattle and sheep and, like all settlers in a new and still largely unexplored land, they erected stockades to protect their homesteads against predators: the wolf, the lynx and the fox. These first farmers believed in an after-life and they left behind them over three hundred megalithic tombs containing deposits of pottery and flint heads, part of the grave-goods they buried with their dead.

In time a second and more sophisticated group of settlers would overlap with the first farmers, who were simpler folk. This second group, known as the passage-grave builders, is still an enigma and a source of wonder to us. Not only were they farmers and skilled builders but they appear to have had a knowledge of astronomy amazing for their period. They left behind them burial chambers at Newgrange, Knowth and Dowth in the Boyne valley. Newgrange, the best-known, is one of the oldest buildings in the world, so constructed that after a lapse of five and a half thousand years it is as waterproof as the day it was built. It is awe-inspiring with its intricately carved stones, burial-chamber and cremation basins which once held the ashes of dead kings and princes. The narrow fanlight above the main entrance doorway was so designed that the sunlight shines up the passage and into the chamber, filling the place with golden light at the dawn of the winter solstice, 21 December, proof that these mysterious people believed that there was a spirit world and that the dead returned.

The early farmers who came to our shores were the first of a succession of immigrants and invaders who were to shape the history of Ireland and to lay the foundations for a way of life, strands of which have lasted down to our own times. Stone Age man would give way to men of the Bronze Age and would in the course of time be succeeded by men of the Iron Age. It was towards the end of the Bronze Age, around 500 BC, that the Celts began to arrive and it is safe to say that they were settled here in the first century AD.

Some time around 500 BC there was a climatic change to the cool, moist sub-Atlantic conditions that prevail today—conditions ideal for the introduction of a new crop, namely oats. By the time we come to the period known as Early Christian Ireland we find a settled, well-organised community, pastoral to a remarkable degree. Wheat, barley, oats and rye were grown, but cattle were the cornerstone of the economy. The basic unit of value and exchange was the cow: a bondsman's worth was four cows. Wealth was reckoned not so much in broad acres as in herds of cattle. Cattle raids were less a method of warfare than a sortie into another tribe's territory in which a young man might test his manhood. They were also part of the ceremonial inauguration of a prince or chieftain. Indeed such common occurrences were they that they are mentioned on no less than 402 occasions in the *Annals of Ulster*. It is little wonder that a cattle raid forms the basis of our greatest saga, the *Táin Bó Cuailgne*—Cattle Raid of Cooley. It is from such mythological and legendary stories, as well as from folklore, fable and archaeological remains, that we can piece together a picture of how our ancestors lived.

Our knowledge of the foods our ancestors ate comes mainly from archaeological remains, written sources, early Irish laws, legendary stories that describe great feasts and hunting sagas, lives of the saints, and tales told by princes, poets and prelates, historians, antiquarians, soldiers of fortune, early tourists to our shores, and oral sources, commonly referred to as *folklore*.

Hunting was a favourite pastime in early Ireland, and the remains of outdoor cooking places used by hunters, some dating back to pre-Christian Ireland, are still to be seen in parts of Connacht and Munster. They are usually found near water—streams, wells or rivers—and consist of a boiling-pit, a roasting-pit, a hearth for a fire, and a wattle hut for storing food. They are traditionally associated with Fionn and the Fianna, a legendary band of heroes who were reputed to live in Ireland about the 3rd century AD, and are known to this day as *fulachtaí Fiann* (cooking-pit of the Fianna) or *fulachtaí fia*.

For countless generations the food Irish people ate was wholesome and nutritious. Rivers and seas gave great harvests of fish: salmon was a particular favourite, cōsting little or nothing. Milk, butter, cheese and cream were plentiful: indeed there were twenty different sorts of white-meats (milk products). Most households kept a pig, so that pork, fresh and salted, home-cured hams, puddings and sausages were plentiful. While ducks, geese and hens were popularly eaten and are mentioned in the early literature and in folk-tales, the turkey, like the potato, did not make an appearance until Elizabethan times. It took another couple of centuries, however, for the potato to become part of the staple diet of the Irish. In the 12th and 13th centuries the Normans introduced not only rabbits and fallow deer but also sycamores and other trees from Europe. Vegetables were used mainly as a condiment or dressing with meats or in salads. From Norman times on, peas and beans became an important supplement to a diet which had its basis in milk foods.

The markets of medieval Dublin offered strawberries, raspberries, damsons, sloes, cherries and blackberries from field banks; bilberries or fraughans from the slopes of the Dublin hills; the pears and plums and apples so often mentioned in early sagas and imported luxuries like almonds, figs, raisins and walnuts from the spice ships of southern Europe. The Smock Alley and Aungier Street playhouses of 18th-century Dublin resounded to the cries of the street girls hawking their wares in the theatre pit: "Who will buy my sweet juicy oranges?" The cries of the fishmongers heard in Norse Dublin are echoed today in the street markets of Moore Street: "Fish, fresh fish."

Dr Massari was the secretary of Archbishop Rinuccini, who in 1645 was appointed Nuncio Extraordinary to the ill-fated Confederation of Kilkenny. From the letters he wrote back to Italy we get a vivid picture of life in Ireland and of how well the common people ate. Fish was plentiful; oysters cost little; there was an abundance of milk, butter and cheese, while apples, pears, plums and cherries grew in profusion. The letters reveal how cheaply all victuals were sold.

From prehistoric times up to the end of the 17th century corn and milk were the mainstay of most of the population. Wheat, oats, rye and barley were grown, but oats was the chief crop, and oaten bread and porridge were widely used. Every farmhouse made butter and cheeses, both hard and soft. Great quantities of curds were eaten and whey drunk; sweet milk, thick milk, buttermilk and sour milk formed part of every meal. Households brewed their own beer and ale; wine was made from flowers and fruit. Honey was the chief sweetening agent, and formed the basis of mead, a drink both potent and popular, until the general acceptance of sugar in the 17th and 18th centuries.

Fine wines were imported from early times, coming the long sea routes from Italy and France. The first mention of whiskey appears in the *Annals of Clonmacnoise*, under the year AD 1405. Ireland had a long and distinguished reputation for distilling the best whiskey in these islands.

Undoubtedly the finest single record of food eaten in medieval Ireland is contained in the 12th-century poem *Aisling Meic Con Glinne*—The Vision of Mac Conglinne—a story about a hungry scholar from Armagh who sets out to visit the greatest gourmandiser in Ireland, King Cathal Mac Finguine of Munster. In the course of his travels the scholar has a Hansel-and-Gretel-type dream or vision of a land of plenty. He mentions such foods as wheaten bread and salmon, smoky bacon gammon, tender mutton, beef, cheese, carrots, kale, whortleberries and hazelnuts, and describes a butter mountain, a lake of milk and a moat of custard which guards the entrance to a castle of meat with a roof of sausages and puddings.

Behind the castle are a fountain of ale and a wood of sweet apples. The most delectable drink in the Land of Plenty is milk. Mac Conglinne rhapsodises about "very thick milk, milk not too thick, milk of long thickness, milk of medium thickness, yellow bubbling milk, and milk the swallowing of which needs chewing."[1] It is also interesting to read how Mac Conglinne cures the king of his demon of gluttony, first by forcing Cathal to fast and then by feeding him on a diet of new milk, fresh butter and honey boiled together.

Three events were eventually to reshape the traditional diet of the Irish. The Norman invasion of the 12th century brought with it a new pattern of eating with a dependence on cereals, beans, peas and bread. From prehistoric times the old Irish had relied heavily on milk—liquid, solid and semi-solid. This had its roots in animal husbandry. But gradually the two patterns merged. Beans and peas preserve well and supplement a grain diet. Supported by milk, butter and beef in the summer months, the Irish now had an all-year-round food supply.

The second change came about by the late 17th century with the widespread adoption of the potato, a change which was to have such a cataclysmic effect not only on the eating habits but on the entire way of life of a people. Foods which had been widely used for a thousand years or more were forgotten, and a country that had fed well on milk produce, corn and meat now grew dependent on the potato. It could be argued that the people as a whole were healthy. If a man ate some 10 pounds of potatoes a day, comp-lemented with milk at each meal and the occasional helping of fish or meat, he was well nourished, with sufficient protein, calcium, iron and calories. But it was life lived at the knife-edge of disaster. There had been potato famines before 1845–47 and would be later, but when the potato means the difference between life and death, a blight occurring for three consecutive years spells ruination and death to millions.

The third change in the eating pattern was insidious and came about almost unnoticed with the introduction of tea and white bread in the late 19th century.

Many writers and students of ethnology and folk-life have observed that people are extremely conservative in the foods they eat. Changes in the pattern of diet are slow, and it may appear an oversimplification to seem to date so precisely these three changes. Men and women, young and old, rich and poor may eat differently. Even families are often divided in their eating habits. The foods available, the seasons of the year, the amounts of money on hand, custom, habit, travel, religious beliefs—all play a part.

It is interesting to note that even in the mid-19th century when so many were dependent on the potato crop and living at bare subsistence level, workmen and servants employed by the more substantial farmers or in the Big Houses, ate very well indeed. Andrew J Kettle, a gentleman farmer wo owned a substantial holding at St Margaret's in north Co Dublin, describes the food eaten on the farm in the years immediately preceding the Great Famine of 1845–47:

> The food was nearly all home-made; wholemeal bread, oaten meal flour, ground on the farm made into stirabout, potatoes all floury, first quality butter, bacon raised, killed and cured on the premises, milk unadulterated *ad libitum* for everyone and everything, and honey bees in almost every garden...I often held the scale for my grandmother to weigh a pound of bacon for each workman's dinner, three days a week, with a quarter of fresh mutton and four duck eggs on the other days. No tea, not much butcher's meat, unless at Christmas and Easter, but plenty of pork steaks at the pig killing periods and the best of pigs' puddings and sausages.[2]

A study of traditional food has to do not only with the ingredients used but with methods of cooking and preserving. Before the advent of refrigerators and freezing cabinets, people had their own methods, relying on salt, herbs or bog-holes to preserve food.

One English commentator in the reign of Charles II noted: "Butter was mixed with garlic and buried in a bog to give it a high taste for Lent."[3] A bog hole or a house built with flagstones on the mountain tops, so that it resembled an ice-house, might be used to store butter; neither rain nor wind could get inside and the butter would be preserved perfectly until taken down and sold at the markets. "Salted" butter, or "country" butter as it was known, was commonly used up to the end of the 1940s. Meat was also salted and buried in bog-holes. It was said that the bog-water preserved the meat. Up to recent times ice was packed and sold for preservation purposes. An account from the archives of the Department of Irish

Folklore, University College, Dublin, describes how when the snow
fell on the Macgillycuddy Reeks in Co Kerry, groups of men and
boys would climb to where the snow lay thick and fill baskets and
small wooden forms, box-shaped, like brick moulds. They would
beat the snow into the moulds until it was "hard as a rock" and
pack the iced lumps. These were rushed to Killorglin and sold to
the salmon fishery. Corned beef was a festive dish; bacon was cured
by salting and hanging the flitch over a fire, preferably of greenwood.
Ling, cod and other white fish were salted and hung in the rafters
until needed, then taken down and cooked. Smoked salmon was
used from early times.

Even the manner and times of eating meals changed over the
centuries. Up to the beginning of the 18th century forks at table
were unknown except in fashionable establishments. The Rev
Caesar Otway in 1698 describes how in an Irish home he ate dinner
with a knife and drank from a wooden noggin, there being no cups[4]
and some years earlier Dinley[5], that noted English commentator on
Irish affairs, observed that the Irish used shells for spoons. The
fashion of using forks became known in England only in the reign
of James I, which fashion had come from Italy to England, and, as
was usual Ireland took its lead from the sister island. In earlier times
dinner was eaten at 11 o'clock in the morning and in the 15th
century it was said that a man who was still in his bed at 6 am was
lazy, half-witted or a gentleman of leisure. Throughout the 17th
century it was customary for the gentry in Ireland to dine at noon
and sup at 7 pm. By the 18th century fashionable folk were dining
at 3 pm, but as the century drew to a close the hour for dining
became later, after the Continental custom, until in the 19th century
dinner was served to the gentry at 7 pm. Humble folk and those
who were not slaves to fashion ate when it suited them to do so:
when the day's work was finished, when they could manage the
time to eat or when beset by the pangs of hunger. John Millington
Synge, who visited the Aran Islands in the early 1900s, noted that
the men of Aran ate a little after dawn before they scattered for their
work but that during the day they simply drank a cup of tea and
ate a piece of bread or some potatoes when hungry.

For men who live in the open air they eat strangely little.[6]

Festivals, weddings, wakes—all had their special foods, richer and more varied than that normally served at table; and many were the rites and prognostications associated with such events. Fairies or people of the Otherworld had to be placated by food offerings, likewise the dead; spells and incantations involving food were used to foretell the future and to ward off hunger for the year to come "Marbhfháisc ar an gcailligh rua"—"Destruction to the red-haired hag" or "Destruction to the red-haired girl"—was a favourite incantation, for she was the popular personification of hunger and famine.

R Sayce, the noted anthropologist, has this to say about the study of food:

> The producing of food is one of the most fundamental of all occupations. It absorbs the greater part of people's energy, helps to determine their social relationships and is a centre about which many of their sentiments are formed.[7]

It can truly be said that any meal, festive or otherwise, eaten in good company, and in congenial surroundings, raises the spirits, improves the digestion and enhances good fellowship as nothing else can.

REFERENCES

1. Kuno Meyer (trans.), *Aisling Meic Con Glinne*—The Vision of Mac Conglinne, London, 1892, 5-113.
2. Andrew J. Kettle, *Material for Victory*, Dublin, 1958, 5.
3. Thomas Dinley, *Tour of Ireland*, *JRSAI* IV, 1856-57.
4. Edward MacLysaght, *Irish Life in the 17th Century*, Dublin, 1939, 255.
5. Dinley, op. cit., 79.
6. J M Synge,*The Aran Islands*, Dublin, 1968, 258.
7. *Béaloideas* XII, 1942, 75-79.

2

A Plenteous Place Is Ireland

Irish hospitality was no myth but a warm and living tradition that went back to pagan times and lasted down to this century. Perhaps the greatest dishonour a person could bring upon himself in pre-Christian Ireland was to be accused of miserliness, niggardliness or refusal to give hospitality. Later Christian thinking dovetailed into the earlier pagan code with its belief in the virtues of liberality towards the poor and needy, as well as obligations towards the guest.

This tradition of goodwill, generosity and gentleness towards all continued to be practised from the 5th century onwards, through centuries of peace and years of strife, through periods of prosperity and dark days of famine, and, what is most remarkable, the warmest hospitality was often to be found in the most miserable cabin. In Irish tradition hospitality was not merely a virtue but an overriding duty. Indeed it could be said that the Irish had an almost superstitious fear of turning the stranger away from the door. Who knew who the stranger might be?

The duties of a husbandman are beautifully expressed in some of the most evocative lines to be found in the early Irish translated by the noted scholar Kuno Meyer:

> Bid thy guests welcome, though they should come at every
> hour

Since every guest is Christ—no trifling saying this;
Better is humility, better gentleness, better liberality towards
    him.[1]

In the old Irish period it was the duty of every free landowner
to receive king, bishop or judge and to prepare his house for the
visits of their company. But the responsibility for dispensing
hospitality rested most heavily on the *brughaidh* or hosteller, as he
was known, usually a wealthy freeman. According to the ancient
laws of Ireland the hosteller must have double the property of a
ruling noble in order to be his equal in dignity. He must keep open
house for all comers, closing the door against none, and he must
keep no reckoning no matter how often a guest chose to come or
how long he stayed. Each hostel must have in readiness a hundred
servants and a hundred domestic animals of each kind: cattle,
swine, horses, sheep, goats, dogs, cats, hens, bees, as well as a
hundred beehives.

Occasionally hospitality was abused, as is shown in the story of
Buchet the *brughaidh*, first written down in the 10th-century *Yellow
Book of Lecan*,[2] but undoubtedly a much more ancient tale. Buchet
was a kindly and generous host whose hospitality was abused by
the twelve profligate brothers of his dearly loved foster-daughter
Eithne. There was not their like in all Ireland for high living and
extravagances and they frequently descended on the unfortunate
Buchet with their servants and retainers, consuming everything
within reach. Before long Buchet was ruined and was forced to sell
his herds and lands and to move to a woodman's cottage near the
seat of the High King at Kells, Co Meath. But like all moral tales
this had a happy ending. King Cormac riding in the forest met the
bewitching Eithne and made her his queen. He gave Buchet the
bride-price of his foster-daughter, including herds of cattle, bronze
cauldrons, and so much gold that Buchet could scarcely carry his
wealth back to his former home. Ever afterwards, the story tells us,
Buchet, who was a dedicated host, continued to keep open house
and each night entertained as many as came. Fifty musicians played
for the guests and there was so much song and music that to this

very day, in folklore, men still speak with wonder of the "melodies of Buchet's House."

In early accounts of saints' lives we find stories of how, because of living a frugal existence or perhaps because of excessive charity, a holy man or woman has nothing with which to entertain an unexpected guest. Usually a miracle is wrought through prayer. A servant catches a very large fish sufficient for the whole company, the cow gives extra milk, meat or drink is somehow provided and dishonour is avoided.

Traditionally the name Guaire is synonymous with hospitality. Another story from the *Yellow Book of Lecan* tells how Guaire, King of Connacht, known as *Guaire an Oinigh*—Guaire the noble or hospitable—was one Easter Sunday served a feast in his palace at Durlas. "Great the bowl of Guaire," the story says, "a pig and a bull calf were put into it". Now the king was a man of modest appetites, who moreover liked to share what he had with those less fortunate. When he saw what had been put on the table before him, he said, "I would be thankful to Christ our Saviour if I could share this food with some hungry person for it is not fitting, even for a king, to eat so much." In answer to his prayer, two angels appeared and bore the table containing the king's dishes westwards to the Burren of Connacht where the hermit Colmán Mac Duach had spent many years in the wilderness fasting on a diet of watercress and herbs of the forest, even refusing an Easter dish of savoury food his clerk had prepared and brought to him.

The hermit was in his refectory when the angels, invisible to human eye, set the table down before him. When his clerk saw this he said to his master, "Well, here is a reward for your abstinence. Eat what God has sent you."

"Not until I know whence it came," said the hermit. Then, put his hands about the bowl praying, "O little bowl, what brought you over the woods of Luaire?"

In answer he heard the angel's voice: "It came because of the liberality of King Guaire." The king had followed on horseback. He asked the holy man how long he had been fasting and was told, "Forty nights and seven years." Then he commanded the hermit:

"Eat the food. It is I, your king, who sent it." And the hermit did as he was bid, praying, "God reward you."

The legend tells us that the next day the king gave the hermit a gift of three score milch cows and three score workmen to build a church in front of the refectory, which was called the church of Mac Duach. And according to the story all the descendants of King Guaire worshipped there and believed till doom.

Down the centuries visitors to Ireland, writers and observers, tourists and even marauders such as the Vikings of the 10th century were astonished at the unsurpassing hospitality of the Irish. In the Icelandic sagas we find an account noted down possibly by a Viking raider of how the Irish built their houses at crossroads in order to encourage travellers to come in and eat with them. What is still more strange, the men from the north were so intrigued with this custom that they introduced it to Iceland when they got back home.

Gaelic society was in essence rural, based on agriculture and the system of barter. Even with the advent of the Normans in the 12th century, Irish culture, traditions and language continued to flourish and develop side by side with the newer Anglo-Norman life-style. As the saying goes, in time the Normans became more Irish than the Irish themselves. They inherited or adopted the practice of hospitality, and soon were entertaining bards and poets in their great Norman strongholds.

The rights of hospitality in medieval times can be broken down into three main sections: the right of any traveller to food and lodgings; the right of a king or overlord to billet his servants—known as *coshering*—and the right of a lord to be entertained by his vassals.

In the period following the Norman invasion, three classes of men were expected to keep open house as the *Annals* [3] record. The first of these comprised holders of church lands, more especially hereditary churchmen, who might or might not have taken holy orders and who, in return for such privileges, were expected to extend hospitality. The professional class came next: doctors, poets, historians or wealthy craftsmen, all of whom held land free from ordinary taxation and who in return were expected to maintain a guest house and as often as not a bardic school.

The traditional hosteller or hostel-keeper was the third. He corresponded to the *brughaidh* of an earlier age and was nearly always a man of means, but not of the first importance, who sought to buy his way into aristocratic society. His table was usually lavish and he particularly welcomed powerful chieftains, princes and their minions, and influential men of letters. However, any traveller could expect not only free board and lodgings but a warm welcome, be he beggar, wandering student, itinerant musician, juggler, clown, monk, priest or soldier. This was a natural result of the times: bad roads, lack of transport often of any kind, and political fragmentation which made any man a foreigner thirty miles from his native town or village. It was an excellent and praiseworthy way of distributing wealth in the days before the advent of hotels and inns and worked admirably for all. Men of arts and letters, bards, poets and musicians were often the most demanding of guests, the most difficult to please, and many a hostel-keeper or lord of a great house went in dread of being made a subject of mockery in a poem or ballad composed in his dishonour. It was generally held by experienced travellers and knowledgeable guests that food and lodgings and general comforts were best provided when a woman, be she wife or mistress, oversaw the servants and supervised the kitchens.

It is interesting to note that bishops and priests, who were sufficiently conservative in the late Middle Ages to observe the age-old custom of providing hospitality, tended to carry their dislike of all things new to the point of ignoring other changes brought on by 12th-century reforms in the church. Some of them continued, as before, to marry or keep concubines, and to pass on their offices, where possible to their descendants. Men of letters in general approved of their stand, their refusal to bow to new decrees, and indeed it was to their advantage to do so. The younger and more obedient, the more austere and disciplined clergy who accepted new edicts and practised celibacy, no longer kept "open house", or if they did standards of cuisine and comfort fell abysmally. On the other hand in the houses of the more old-fashioned clergy who continued to keep their châtelaines the usual high standards were maintained, a fact which seasoned travellers and professional bards were quick to recognise, approve, and praise in story and song.

Social climbing is no modern phenomenon. Down the centuries men and women have aped those whom they consider their betters, and in every age class rears its ugly head. All men are equal in the eyes of the law, but it is, and always has been, axiomatic that some are more equal than others. One of the most audacious displays of wealth and snobbery in the Ireland of the late Middle Ages occurred, when Margaret, daughter of Ó Cearbhaill and wife of An Calbhach Ó Conchobhair, decided to have "open house" in the famine year of 1435. She issued a general invitation to 2,700 men of arts and letters and arranged to receive them at the great church of Da Sinceall, clad in cloth of gold, with her husband seated on horseback beside her. Some years later Margaret's daughter, Fionnuala, endeavoured to upstage her mother when she and her second husband invited all the poets of Ireland to a banquet no less lavish. Undoubtedly they both got mention in what passed for the gossip columns of the time—a poetic tribute, a ballad written in their honour and no doubt a lot of unfavourable comment from people who were not invited or who accepted the invitation and then mischievously held their hosts up to ridicule.

Perhaps the best-remembered account of a great banquet in the old Irish tradition, and one which went into folk history, was that of Brian na Múrtha Ó Ruairc, who at Christmastide in the year 1591 held "open house" in the great hall of his castle at Dromahair, Co Leitrim. The occasion was later celebrated in the folk song, "Pléaráca na Ruarcach", and still later immortalised by Jonathan Swift, Dean of St Patrick's Cathedral, when in the 18th century he penned the following words to the music of Carolan.

> O'Rourke's noble fare will ne'er be forgot,
> By those who were there, and those who were not.
> His revels to keep, we sup and we dine,
> On seven score sheep, fat bullock and swine.
> Usquebaugh to our feast in pails was brought up,
> A hundred at least, and a madder our cup.
> Oh there is the sport, we rise with the light,
> In disorderly sort, from snoring all night.[4]

It was not only great chieftains and fashionable lords and ladies who liked to dispense hospitality. Dr Massari in 1645 was very impressed by the hospitality of the ordinary people, and wrote:

> The kindness of these poor people among whom the noble lord [Archbishop Rinuccini] had come by chance, was without compare. At once they slaughtered a large ox, two sheep and a pig and brought a plentitude of beer, butter and milk. And those of us who remained in the ship experienced the generosity of these poor fisher people, by getting the finest fish and oysters of huge size in such abundance that no more could be desired.[5]

Even when the old Irish aristocracy were reduced to penury, through plantations and dispossession, they remembered their former state and continued to observe the traditions of hospitality. John Dunton, an eccentric English bookseller who came to Ireland at the end of the 17th century, and who wrote an account of his experiences here, remarks on this as did so many observers and travellers before and after his time. He visited the Liberties of Dublin and was impressed with the thriving industry of the Huguenot community in their weavers' houses, and also inspected St Patrick's Cathedral, Christ Church and Trinity College. But it was when he reached Iar-Chonnacht, now known as Connemara, then remote and inaccessible with few roads and no inns, that he realised how truly hospitable the poor Irish were.

He writes of seeking shelter in a hovel where he was well received. Fresh green rushes were spread on the floor before him. He asked for a drink of water and his hostess poured sour milk into a wooden vessel, cut out of a single piece of wood, and called a meddar (*meadar*). He was distressed when she picked some dirt out of the vessel with her none-too-clean finger; she then carried the meddar outside and milked the cow to make a syllabub. He says:

> I was surprised at the pleasant taste and extraordinary coldness of it, on such an occasion.[6]

He noted with some surprise how good-humoured, open-hearted and merry the native Irish generally were. Sir John Carr, a Devonshire gentleman, and member of the English Bar, who travelled widely for health reasons, and who arrived in Ireland in 1805, remarked on the poverty of the Irish peasant, and criticised many of their customs, including that of waking the dead with food and drink and collecting money in order to have a convivial funeral. Yet he was impressed by the fact that, to the neighbour or stranger, the door was always open and that anyone was welcome to walk into any cabin without ceremony at meal time and eat what was going, though it might only be a dish of potatoes.

Lavish generosity was not by any means confined to the impoverished Irish. 18th-century English travellers in Ireland were continually struck by the extravagant hospitality and conviviality of the hard-drinking, fox-hunting, feckless landlord class. Maria Edgeworth, in her novel *Castle Rackrent*, describes how an improvident Irish gentleman spent his money. Sir Patrick O'Shaughlin kept a continuous round of house parties going, and these were so popular that some of his boon companions from other ascendancy families were prepared to sleep in the chicken house "which Sir Patrick had fitted up for the purpose of accommodating his friends and the public in general, who honoured him with their company unexpectedly at Castle Rackrent,"[7] rather than be left out of the various entertainments.

And the story is told of a certain gentleman in the west of Ireland who when bereft of company would ride out into the highways and byways issuing invitations to any stray travellers to come and join him at dinner and stay the night. There is little doubt that the Anglo-Irish ascendancy class took on much of the colour and customs of the "old" Irish gentry. But, like colonists everywhere, they looked to the mother country, England, and had little in common with their Irish tenants and servants. Many became absentee landlords, or if forced to remain on their estates, wasted their days hunting, cock-fighting, gambling at cards or dice and often literally drinking themselves under the table with their roistering companions. (Downstairs their Irish servants lived a life apart. It was said that a country-house kitchen was open to every passing beggarman, itinerant tradesman or musician and that none left empty-handed.)

However, not all of the "Big Houses" were run-down or carelessly kept. Here and there the gentry ran their establishments in the style of the English great houses, or after the manner of the French court. Mrs Pendarves, who came to Ireland as a young English widow and who later married Dr Delaney, an Irish clergyman and friend of Dean Swift, kept a lively chronicle of her life in Ireland in the mid-18th century. Like most of her compatriots she was enchanted with the informality of Irish hospitality. Guests delighted in the freedom to do as they pleased.

One of the most elegant of the great establishments was Castletown House, Co Kildare, where, according to Mrs Delaney, old Mrs Connolly, widow of the Speaker of the Irish House of Commons, received callers in her drawing-room every morning for four hours. Promptly at 3 o'clock she sat down to dinner with her guests, who numbered anything up to twenty. No fewer than seven courses were served with two substantial dishes on the sideboard. The guests were attended on by numerous Irish servants, ate from magnificent plate and were entertained throughout the meal by the music of French horns.

Mrs Delaney went into society a great deal, entertained and was entertained. Although married to a clergyman of modest means, she was famous for her dinner parties, at which she might serve a first course of fish, meat, fowl, soup, blancmange, cherries and cheese, followed by a second course of turkey, salmon and quails, with accompanying salads and vegetables, followed by fruit in season served, cream and sweetmeats. A table of twenty people at Delville, the Delaneys' Glasnevin residence, was not unusual and dinner was, as often as not, followed by cards or a dance.

The reason that hospitality was so lavish amongst the gentry was threefold: food was cheap, servants plentiful—they could be had for little more than bed and board—and taxes were trifling compared to those in England. But with the passing of the Act of Union in 1800 and the demise of the Irish Parliament much that was gracious and elegant disappeared from town and country. Many people of wealth and fashion left Dublin to retire to their estates, which became increasingly run-down and dilapidated as the 19th century progressed. More left the country for England, taking their capital with them. For many the days of lavish hospitality were at an end.

According to the noted historian LM Cullen[8] the hospitality of the people, both rich and poor, had been commented on patronisingly by outsiders in the late 18th and early 19th centuries and gradually the Irish had become self-conscious and apologetic about it. Yet amongst the common people the custom of keeping open house appears to have continued down into the late 18th and 19th centuries. Arthur Young[9] visited Mac Dermot, Prince of Coolavin, Co Sligo, who, though reduced to penury, kept open house, addressed his visitors with royal condescension and would not allow anyone, even his children, to sit in his presence. Over thirty years later Edward Wakefield, a London land agent and observer of the 19th-century scene, writes:

> The Wexford peasants have a custom when at meals to sit with their doors open which is an invitation to those passing to enter and partake of their homely fare. So innate is their hospitality that the stranger is always welcome.[10]

The Great Famine of 1845–47 was to change everything, and customs and tradition that had survived against all the odds for two thousand years or more were swept away. Never again would unstinted and prodigal hospitality be taken for granted.

The rise of the Irish middle class in the late 19th and early 20th century did nothing to help keep alive the age-old tradition of hospitality. Middle-class people were in the main unsure of themselves, inward-looking, preoccupied with keeping up appearances. Many were only one generation removed from the mud cabins they so despised; they dared not look back but kept their eyes firmly fixed on the English middle classes they so ardently desired to emulate.

But tradition dies hard. Edward MacLysaght tells of a man living at the end of the 19th century in a small house, with little more than a kitchen and parlour, who received every guest with warmth and hospitality. His house was open to all at every season; everything that a guest might need was supplied. He kept a well-stocked cellar, unlocked, for no one need steal what might be had for the asking. And in town and country up to the present day it is considered unlucky to turn a beggar away from the door. Who knows who that beggar might be! Perhaps in welcoming the stranger the householder may be welcoming Mary's Son.

REFERENCES

1. *Ériú* 2, 12.
2. *Ériú* 1, 43.
3. The Four Masters, *The Annals of the Kingdom of Ireland*, John O'Donovan ed., Dublin, 1845-51.
4. Dónal O'Sullivan, *Carolan: The Life and Music of an Irish Harper*, II, 120.
5. Stanislaus Kavanagh OSFC (ed.). *Commentarius Rinuccinianus*, II, Dublin, 1936, 12-20.
6. In Edward MacLysaght, *Irish Life in the 17th Century*, Dublin and Cork, 1939, p.336.
7. Maria Edgeworth, *Castle Rackrent*. Oxford, 1969, 10.
8. LM Cullen, *The Emergence of Modern Ireland*, New York, 1981, 191.
9. Arthur Young, *A Tour in Ireland*, London, 1780, 153.
10. Edward Wakefield, *An Account of Ireland, Statistical and Political*, London, 1812, 18.

3

The Water of Life

Close to Banbridge in Co Down lies the little village of Loughbrickland. About half a mile to the south-east, sheltered by low hills and trees, is Loch Bricleann or Bricriu's Lake, which gives the village its name. The setting takes us back almost two thousand years to one of the most famous stories in the Ulster cycle. It concerns Bricriu, a wealthy and malicious chieftain who decided to give a feast and for that purpose built a house big enough to accommodate the Ulster heroes and their wives. It was truly magnificent, a branch-red dún, with nine rooms overlaid with gold, modelled on the palace at Eamhain Mhacha. The feast was equally sumptuous, consisting of beef broth, roast boar, salmon, honey cakes and many other dishes; to drink the guests had the finest of ale, the choicest of mead and the rarest of wines. Bricriu promised the "hero's portion" to the Red Branch knight who would prove himself the bravest of the company, a challenge which naturally led first to bitter arguments and then to bitter blows. Their host had planned for this. Not for nothing was he named Bricriu Poison-Tongue.

In another story, *The Wooing of Étáin*, which was written down at Clonmacnoise around the year 1000, from oral sources, we read how the High King Eochaidh made a great feast at Tara at which mead, fine wines and barrels of ale were served. These two early tales are interesting because they tell us of the kind of food and drink served at princely banquets. Today royal Tara stands no more. All that remains of what was once the noblest residence in Ireland is a windswept hill, where archaeologists trace the outlines of the palace, and folk tales keep alive the memory of the mead banqueting-hall, where according to legend the heroes quaffed their favourite brew.

Mead was long a favourite drink, said to be both potent and delicious. It was made from honey, clear sparkling water and aromatic plants. Bragget, made by fermenting ale and honey together, was also much enjoyed for it is frequently mentioned in medieval records. Bees were kept in very great numbers, and to have a surplus of honey for mead-making was highly desirable; districts that produced mead in quantity were lauded by the poets. St Brigid, that redoubtable woman who knew how to influence prelates and princes, is said to have given the King of Leinster a cup of mead to drink when he came to visit her convent. It was of unsurpassing quality and no doubt very potent to boot. Probably as a result of her hospitality she was given a tract of land or some gift she needed for her work amongst the sick and needy. She was noted for the excellence of her kitchen, and had the reputation of brewing the best ale in Ireland. But she was not the only one of the early saints who kept a good cask or two. St Patrick had his favourite brewer who travelled Ireland with him on his missionary work.

Anyone who wished to do so was free to brew his own ale, but the Brehon laws laid down regulations for the sale of ale and for the proper running of ale-houses. Early monastic settlements were sizeable, including, as they did, not only the refectory, kitchens and dormitories for the monks but workshops, bakeries, and accommodation to house lay workers and their families, visiting penitents, students, and indeed anyone who might seek shelter. Regulations which governed everything from the hour of rising of the community to the hour when the weary monk might retire to his cell gave it as a rule of thumb that on days of high feasting laymen and clerics should get equal quantities of food, but that the tonsured monk should get only half as much ale to drink as his brother in the laity.

Much of the early ale was made from malted grain—oats, wheat or barley—together with spring water and honey. Before the introduction of hops in the 16th century, beer, like ale, made with a simple infusion of fermented malt, might be flavoured with aromatic and astringent plants. Oak bark is said to have been used for this purpose, as well as buck beans found in the neighbourhood of certain raths. It was not until around 1780 that beer began to be produced on a commercial scale by small breweries, made from a mixture of malt, grain, water, sugar, yeast and hops. In earlier times the words *ale* and *beer* were often synonymous. The Irish also drank a cider called *nenadmin* made from wild or crab apples, and a drink called *fraochán* made from whortleberries or blackberries.

Perhaps the drink best remembered in folklore is the famous heather ale, a legacy of the years when the long-prowed Viking ships raided Irish waters, and a simple monk whose name we shall never know wrote on the margin of the manuscript he was illustrating one stormy winter night:

> Fierce and wild is the wind tonight;
> It turns the tresses of the sea to white;
> On such a night as this I take my ease;
> Fierce Northmen only course the quiet seas.[1]

The story goes that the Vikings or Danes, as they are traditionally known, were superb brewers of beer, but their heather ale was unsurpassed; the recipe, a carefully guarded secret, was handed down from father to son. After the Battle of Clontarf in 1014, when the power of the Danes in Ireland was finally broken and the foreigners driven into the sea, only one family escaped. They were taken captive by an Irish chieftain near the Cliffs of Moher in Co Clare and were offered their lives in exchange for the secret of the brew. "I would be ashamed to tell you before my son," the fierce old Dane said, and watched unmoved as the young man was put to the sword. He then led his captor to the edge of the cliff and whispered long and earnestly in the other's ear.

"And is that all there is to it? The special herbs and the manner of brewing?" The chieftain hugged the old man in delight. "You have bought your life; you are free to go."

But at this the Dane tightened his grip. "Had my son lived he might have bartered the secret for his life, but now you and I alone know how the heather ale is made and we shall take that knowledge with us to our doom." And with those words the Dane jumped over the cliff, taking the Irish chieftain with him to a watery grave far below. And so was lost for ever the secret of the heather ale.

We may safely assume that by the 12th century there were many places in Ireland which enjoyed the reputation of making excellent ales and many a man who had a good palate for a fine wine. Even in early times there was considerable trade with the Continent. Furs and hides were exported to Gaul, and back came cargoes of wine, so that amongst wealthy merchants and princelings it was a well-known drink.

One of the most enigmatic anecdotes of the year AD 535 tells of dark passions and a woman betrayed. It appears that the palace of Cletty was set on fire by a certain beautiful lady, who had been scorned by the king, while the members of the court were at table. "To escape the flames," the record says, "the king plunged into a vat of wine but was drowned." And so the lady was avenged; but there the record ends, and we shall never know the fully story. Was there a still more beautiful rival for the king's heart involved, or a jealous wife waiting in the wings, or even a distracted husband who had refused to play cuckold any longer and was bent on revenge? What subsequently happened the dark lady? Did she enter a nunnery? Placate her husband as so many women before and since have done? Did she lie awake at night weeping over her dead love or did she put the past behind her? One thing is certain, human nature never changes, and crimes of passion happen in every stratum of society and in every age.

Giraldus Cambrensis, or Gerald the Welshman, who visited Ireland in the 12th century and who wrote what is probably the first travel book about the island, commented on the abundance of wine imported into the country from Poitou, France. A story is told of how in the 13th century a Munster chieftain, one Amhlaoibh Ó hEidirsceoil was given his nickname. One day, as a young boy, he was down at the harbour, watching the ships and dreaming of far distant lands as young boys do, when he was abducted by a rival chieftain and handed over to the crew of a wine ship from Gascony as a pledge of payment for a cargo. He was taken to France and put to work in the vineyards, thereby giving credence to the old belief that fruit grew without blemish if the vines were tended by those of noble blood. Later the youth was brought back to Ireland and ever afterwards bore the nickname "the Gascon."

Wine and ale flowed freely at great feasts given by princes and chieftains. A scribe named Muirchú writing in the 7th century describes how St Patrick came to the palace of King Laoghaire at Tara on Easter Sunday in the year of Our Lord 433. There he found kings, princes and druids feasting and drinking wine. From what we know of Patrick, he probably joined the company in the spirit of good will, before setting about converting the pagans. This custom seems not to have changed down the years. A 13th-century poem speaks of the bard going from "one feast of purple wine to another."

However, not all drink consumed was come by honestly. Not infrequently the Irish levied "blacks rents" on the Pale of Dublin and surrounding districts. In 1444 Eoghan O'Neill, Lord of Tyrone, plundered the town of Dundalk, and demanded sixty marks and two tons of wine in return for not destroying the town by fire— a demand that was quickly met by the frightened townsfolk.

By the 16th century cheap, low-quality wine had become more readily available, especially around coastal waters where Spanish and English merchant seamen traded wine, beer and bales of silk for hides, fish, salt and meat. Sometimes it was a case, not of honest trading but of treacherous intents. We read of English merchant ships arriving in ports with cargoes of fine wines and encouraging Irish chieftains to imbibe, not wisely but too well, while their followers, left leaderless, were routed by the enemy army—much the same technique as was employed by Elizabeth's minions when the captain of the decoy ship at Lough Swilly invited the young

Aodh Ruadh Ó Dónaill aboard at Christmas 1587, made him drunk on wine and took him in chains to Dublin Castle.

Fynes Moryson, that inveterate traveller and historian who came to Ireland as Lord Mountjoy's secretary in 1600 and remained with Mountjoy all through the long and bitter campaign which ended with the defeat of the great Hugh O'Neill, kept a record of his time here, entitled *The Commonwealth of Ireland*. He wrote that when the common Irish have money to spend they like to imbibe freely:

> Whenever they come to a market town to sell a cow or a horse they never return home until they have drunk the price in Spanish wine, which they call the "King of Spain's daughter."[2]

A brisk trade in smuggling wine and fine brandy along the western seaboard and around the coast of Kerry lasted until well into the 19th century. After the defeat of Patrick Sarsfield and the signing of the Treaty of Limerick in 1691, a treaty which was broken ere the ink was dry, many of the old Irish aristocracy with their retainers fled the country for ever. Following them went the soldiers who had fought with Sarsfield, each man with a price on his head. The ships that took the Wild Geese as the members of the Irish Brigade came to be known on the battlefields of Europe, often engaged in a two-way smuggling exercise, running in wine and spiriting out wanted men.

Smuggling was a hazardous occupation, and the culprit if caught risked a penalty that might mean death or at least transportation for life; but for some it was a way of surviving and even of amassing a fortune. Others in coastal districts engaged in ship-wrecking, luring ships to their doom on treacherous rocks and scavenging what the sea gave up. The fame and wealth of many an Irish family, such as the O'Connells of Derrynane, Co Kerry, the household that bred the Liberator, Daniel O'Connell, was founded on smuggling.

It is no exaggeration to say that since the late Middle Ages when the art of distilling became known in these parts, Irish whiskey has always been rated the best there is. Time and again writers and travellers to our shores have commented on the excellence of our *aqua vitae*, or to give it the old Irish title, *uisce beatha*, meaning "water of life", which was indeed how many people regarded it.

In folk tales a popular motif is where the hero is put under *geasa* or bonds to undertake a journey to the Well at the World's End, or some other such mythical place, in search of the water of life. His journey is fraught with dangers, he performs incredible feats of valour, is often helped by fabulous animals or magical old men or women and finally succeeds in his quest and is rewarded with the hand of a princess in marriage. In all such tales we are told that the "water of life"cures all ills, but more than that, it restores youth, vigour and beauty to the old, the decrepit and the ugly.

It is perhaps no surprise to learn that our early whiskey was indeed used to cure illness and to invigorate the weak and low-spirited. It is not known for certain when the first Irish whiskey was distilled, but we do know that from the 15th century onwards it supplemented wine and beer.

The art of distilling spirits is believed to have been discovered in the 11th century in Mediterranean countries and was at first chiefly used for curative purposes. No authentic record exists to show when it first reached Ireland, or if, indeed, it was independently discovered. Possibly Irish monks returning from sojourns abroad brought back with them a knowledge of distillation. In those days monasteries ran hospices for the care of the sick and needy, and a newly discovered drink that was both palatable and had remedial uses would have an immediate appeal.

Edward Campion in his *History of Ireland* (1633), speaking of a famine which was said to have taken place three hundred years earlier, says it was caused by soldiers eating flesh and drinking *aqua vitae* in Lent; and in another place he mentions a Norman baron preparing an army to fight the Irish about 1350, and allowing every soldier, before he buckled with the enemy, a mighty draught of the same drink. It is possible that the drinks mentioned may have been old ale.

The first authentic record of whiskey was recorded in the *Annals of the Four Masters* under the year of Our Lord 1405, when it stated that a certain Risteard Mac Raghnaill, heir to the chieftainship of Muintir Eolais, died on Christmas Day of a surfeit of *aqua vitae*. To which brief note the scribe, one Mageoghagan, appends a wry footnote: "Mine author says it was not to him *aqua vitae*, but *aqua mortis*."[3]

By the time Elizabeth I came to the throne of England, Irish whiskey was both widely known and appreciated, as is evident from commentators of the period.

It seems to have been something of a liqueur whiskey, well sweetened and flavoured with a variety of ingredients, including raisins, dates, liquorice, aniseed and various herbs—the flavours depending on the demands made on the distiller and the taste of the imbiber.

A recipe for making Irish whiskey, dated 1602, is interesting if only for the various ingredients listed.

> To every gallon of good aqua composita, add two ounces of liquorice, bruised and cut into small pieces; add two ounces of aniseed, cleaned and bruised. Let them macerate for five or six days in a wooden vessel, stopping the same close, and then draw off as much as will run clear, dissolving in that clear aqua vitae, five or six spoonfuls of the best molasses you can get; then put this in another vessel, and after three or four days, when the liquer hath fined itself, you may use same. Add dates and raisins to this recipe. The grounds which remain you may redistill and make more aqua composita of them and out of that you may make more usquebaugh.[4]

Usquebaugh or Irish whiskey continued to be drunk not only for its excellent taste and as an aid to conviviality but as a cure for all ills. Fynes Moryson, who could be disparaging about Irish diet in general, credited Irish whiskey as "the best drink of its kind in the world". He recommended it as a drink which loosens the bowels, binds up the belly and dries up moisture, without inflaming any parts. He continues to sing its praises thus:

> The Irish aqua vitae, commonly called usquebaugh is also made in England, but nothing so good as that which is brought out of Ireland. And the usquebaugh (or Irish whiskey) is preferred before our aqua vitae because of the mingling of saffron, raisins, fennel seed and other things, mitigating the heat and making the taste pleasant and refreshing to the weak stomach.[5]

Not only was Irish whiskey enjoyed and appreciated at home but it was frequently sent to persons of quality in England, either as a rare cordial or as something better than they could procure locally. As was to be expected with such a superior product, lesser men might use it as a bribe, or at least as a means of ingratiating themselves with those in high places. In the State Papers Office there is a letter from Mayor White of Waterford to Lord Burghley, dated 1585, describing gifts sent to his lordship consisting of two bed coverings, two green mantles and a roundell of aqua vitae.

Whatever about the lower orders being forced to make do with ale, beer or cheap wine, Irish whiskey had become a favourite tipple with the more affluent by the end of the 16th century. A traveller to Ireland, one William Lithgow, who lived between 1586 and 1645, wrote of his visit to this country:

> Gentlemen of good sort, and indeed all other authorities, ever reserve stores of Spanish sack and Irish usquebaugh, and will be as typsy with their friends and priests as though they were naturally in the eleven royal taverns of Naples.[6]

In 1581, Derricke praised Irish whiskey in verse:

> Again if fortune faunt, or on them chance to smile
> She fills them up with usquebaugh and wine another while.
> Oh that is cheer in bowls, it beautifies the feast

And makes them look most drunkenly from most unto the
least.[7]

A traveller who visited Ireland in 1579 commented on the
scarcity of inns, but added:

Outside the port town there are no lodging houses to be
found, but any traveller is welcome to put up in any house
he meets, where he is warmly received and entertained
without payment. The table is not usually laid until evenings,
when the meal is served but in the meantime drink is not
denied the traveller. There are eight sorts of draught on
offer: beer made of barley and water, milk, whey, wines,
broth, mead, usquebaugh and spring water.[8]

As early as 1580 the authorities in England complained about
the abuse of drink by the Irish, asserting that spirit drinking was
causing unrest amongst the natives. Directives were issued that
martial law be applied to idle persons and makers of *aqua vitae*.[9]

More than half a century later, Sir William Petty, one of the most
successful of the Cromwellian adventurers, enriched by confiscation
of Irish lands, a doctor of medicine, and benefactor to Ireland by
reason of his *Survey of the Political and Economic State of the Country*,
gave some startling figures. In Dublin, he found, there were no
fewer than 1,180 ale-houses and 91 public houses— nearly one-third
of the total number of houses—catering for a population of around
4,000 families. He also found that about 1,800 women and servants
were engaged in the trade of drink.

It is interesting to note that Dr Petty carried out his survey in
a large house in Crow Street, Dublin, which house was later to
become a Protestant orphanage, and was known as the "Crow's
Nest."Up to the early years of the present century many Dublin
Catholics had a superstitious fear of the "Crow's Nest", believing
that Catholic orphans were taken into the home and proselytised.

Industry and diligence were marked characteristics of the Irish
in the 17th century, owing to the fact that penal laws had not yet

been introduced and that farmers were reasonably secure in their tenant rights. Yet over-indulgence in drink already presented a problem. In 1645 a commentator said that drunkenness was the only curse of the country... and that "the drinking of usquebaugh and aqua vitae was extraordinary."[10] It was noted that the country was full of houses where drink could be obtained. An act passed that year attempted to curb the excessive number of ale-houses. However, it appears that this act was not strictly enforced or indeed, more likely, that it was unworkable. In *Butler's Journey Through Fermanagh in 1760* we read:

> At Callyhill, John Emmery has a seat. It lies a small distance to the left of the great road in a fine and sporting country. There are neither inns nor alehouses on the road, yet almost every house has for public sale aqua vitae or whiskey which is greatly esteemed by the inhabitants as a wholesome diuretic. They take it before meals, and what is surprising is that they will drink it to intoxication and are never sick after it.

Whiskey had been almost totally a non-commercial beverage for nigh on three hundred years, used in the beginning for medicinal purposes and later to ensure good cheer when fortune smiled or as the laws of hospitality decreed. However, by the middle of the 18th century commercial whiskey began to emerge and, perhaps because the Irish palate had been accustomed to the earlier, richly flavoured whiskey, punch was soon a favourite drink. It was made, as it is today, with whiskey and hot water, flavoured with lemon, cloves, nutmeg or other spices and sweetened with honey or sugar. Punch was reputed to be excellent for a variety of ailments and an unfailing protection against the damp of an Irish climate. It was the favourite tipple of the landlord classes and was soon taken up by strong farmers, shopkeepers and the clergy. Time and again Amhlaoibh Ó Súilleabháin, who was frequently invited to the festive board of the local parish priest or some well-to-do neighbour in the 1820s, describes how the meal was invariably rounded off with plenty of port and hot punch.[11]

Perhaps because it promised not only good cheer but was recommended for health reasons, or because it was drunk in the best houses, or for whatever reason, Irish whiskey was considered a very respectable drink. In answer to a questionnaire on drinks issued by the Department of Irish Folklore UCD, a favourite saying in Listowel, Co Kerry was quoted: "No respectable man or his wife would have the house without it [whiskey], not only to entertain their friends but as a saviour against chills." A "drop of the cratur" was always kept in a cupboard for special occasions. It was referred to as "the priest's bottle" or "the priest's drop" because a glass of whiskey was invariably offered to visiting clergy. Whiskey was the one drink produced at the match-making, when the dowry was settled on and negotiations successfully completed. Whiskey was drunk at weddings, christenings, wakes and at the ball night of the Stations when mass was celebrated in some local house. A substantial breakfast was served to the priest, the household and friends, and all the neighbours were invited in that evening for a ball or party. Whiskey was produced for yearly letting of land and for land sales, when the owners and buyers were treated to drinks. It flowed at American wakes or *conveys*, parties given before the young people left to emigrate to America. In the questionnaire replies we find a poignant description of what took place:

> All the friends and neighbours gathered in the house before the emigrant left and a group of them conveyed him part of the road when the hour of departure dawned. A glass of whiskey was put in his hands with the words, 'Here's your health and may our blessing go with you every step of the way.'…. It would be a poor convey that would not be drunk and crying before 4 am.[12]

In days gone by emigration was a heartbreak to those left at home. The sea journey was arduous and long and the emigrant often unskilled and poorly equipped for the life before him, having little to offer except his health and youth and a will to succeed.

Parents said good-bye to sons and daughters in the almost certain knowledge that they would never again meet in this world. It was a kind of death farewell.

No wake, as the laying out of the corpse was called, was complete without a barrel of porter and a few gallons of whiskey or poteen. Friends and neighbours for miles around would call to the house of mourning when the day's work was complete, to say a prayer, shake holy water on the corpse and sympathise with the family. Then, duty done, they would enjoy themselves, gossiping, playing the traditional and ancient wake games: "spin the bottle, "the priest of the parish has lost his considering cap", forfeits and many more. Snuff and clay pipes were handed around to the men and the older women, and food and drink were provided for all. At the funeral the last lament of the keeners or mourners was "God be with you to God's house, and I'll go to John Johnnies" (the name of the local public house).

Whiskey was always drunk at the traditional *éirí amach* or as it was known in English, coming-out Sunday or show-off Sunday. This referred to the custom of the newly-weds making their public appearance at last mass on the second Sunday following the wedding. For the occasion the bride was decked out in her finery. Long ago when a woman got married she brought with her a chest containing the bed-linen she had woven and possibly a dowry. Her husband purchased her trousseau after the wedding. The newly-weds with their friends and relations adjourned to the local public house or tavern for what was known as the bride's drink. In addition to whiskey, porter, wine and non-alcoholic drinks, ham sandwiches and cakes were served. If the wedding took place immediately before Lent, the bride's drink was postponed until St Patrick's Day.

Fisherman set great store by whiskey and always kept a bottle in the house. It could be a life-saver to a man returning home in the cold dawn, drenched to the skin from a night's fishing. Wisely enough, fisherfolk never took whiskey to sea with them. They needed all their wits to navigate the frail curachs in stormy weather.

Whiskey and porter or stout were provided by farmers for

neighbours who helped at turf-cutting, threshing, hay-making, sheep-shearing and for harvest suppers. At fairs and markets when the day's business was complete—the men having sold their cattle and the women their fowl, butter and eggs—it was usual to adjourn to the local hostelry, where women drank hot claret and men whiskey or stout. In the days of horse-drawn cabs it was usual in town and country to stop at a tavern or public house for refreshments on the way home from a funeral. While the men adjourned to the pub for their glass of whiskey or stout, trays of hot claret, port wine or sherry wine was handed in through the window of the cab to the waiting women, who remained seated in comfort, whiling away the time, sipping and reminiscing about the dead.

Poteen-making can be said to date from the 17th century, when duty was imposed on the distillation of spirits. It was not a sudden change but came about by degrees as the still licence duty rose. At the beginning of the 18th century three classes of persons were allowed to distil spirits: certain householders who could make whiskey for their own use, tavern or inn keepers who could distil for the use of the customers, and specialist distillers who served the public at large. By the second half of the 18th century, the illicit distiller was being driven from town and hamlet to operate in safety in some remote place where he might go undetected: a mountainy area or cave, a place well hidden by rocks, or open bogland where it was difficult for revenue officers to approach unobserved. The needs of the poteen-maker were simple: a nearby stream to supply water, plenty of turf or peat to fire the still, apparatus that was simple and easily moved in case of sudden raids, and the ingredients used in the making of poteen: malt, grain, potatoes, sugar, treacle, molasses, yeast. While modern methods of distilling poteen may be more sophisticated, the technique was relatively simple throughout the 18th and 19th centuries.

Shebeens or illicit liquor-shops, usually smoke-filled, were part of the illegal distilling scene up to the early part of the present century, often advertising their wares by means of a sod of turf hanging above the door. They figured in popular literature, and a shebeen, the home of Pegeen Mike, was immortalised in J M

Synge's classic play, *The Playboy of the Western World*.

Parts of the western seaboard, stretching from Clare to Donegal, maintained a strong tradition of poteen-making, though from a questionnaire issued by the Department of Irish Folklore in 1975 it would appear that poteen was either still being made, or had been made in living memory in more than half of the 26 counties of the Republic. Sligo was at one time a noted centre, and Lisadell a clearing ground, for poteen run in from the island of Innishmurray, just five miles from the coast, a place where large quantities were made. In Kerry, the tradition of poteen-making is best remembered around the Dingle Peninsula, likewise in Drimoleague, Co Cork. Poteen was plentiful in Bantry, and in Cork it was said to have been taken in great quantities to cure aches and pains—indeed any excuse was good enough. In Corcomrua, Co Clare, they remembered the days when poteen was readily available; some of the best was made locally at the Hag's Head.

At one time poteen was brought from the Aran Islands, taken to Doolin, Co Clare, and distributed in the neighbouring districts. There was great intercourse between Inisheer and Liscannor for fishing, particularly during pattern times (feasts of local saints when the pattern was held) and other festive occasions: St Brigid's Day 1 February ; the eve of Garland Sunday (the last Sunday in July); and Lady's Day (15 August) which was a popular local holiday. In Connemara, poteen was brought in by the islanders in exchange for lambs, asses and produce of various kinds. Around Spiddal, Co Galway, people boasted that poteen was to be found on the table of both priest and doctor, which was a tribute both to the quality of the drink and its total acceptability. It was also to be found at weddings and wakes, and plenty was drunk during pattern days.

Mayo always had a strong tradition of poteen-making. Here, as in other parts, they spilled the first run on the ground, to placate the fairies or Good People (the more prosaic reason was that the first run of poteen can be poisonous). This custom of spilling the first three drops of any drink, be it wine, milk or poteen, is very old and was almost universal at one time. In pre-Christian times the libation was often made to the "unknown god".

Inishkeel, Co Donegal, was once a known centre for the making of poteen. An account from the manuscript material reads:

> Poteen was very plentiful long ago, and some is still to be found here and there, made with corn, sugar, treacle and sometimes potatoes. It was soaked in yeast and when it had been soaking for about a week it would take effect. Then it was boiled in the still and strained a few times until it was like clear water. The first time it was drained it was called *singlings*. It was called *kilty* when it was soaking. [13]

A fine account of a poteen-maker, long since gone to his reward, comes from Clonderala, Co Clare.

> Poteen Hill is west of Labasheeda and it is there that Michael Ruadh lived—the best distiller in Clare. He had a copper worm and not many people had that. He had the finest tasting poteen and he made many a drop and many a quart at the foot of the hill. He used keep the still hidden and would put a good cover over the copper worm in a barrel of water: old cans and a few noggins; sugar, corn, malt and fermented worts [completed his store]. There would be a small fire under the still of water and the right heat in the water while the poteen was coming down through the worm. When the first run of poteen was ready he would put it aside in a container or small vessel and would continue distilling until he had the best of poteen. He usually filled two kegs and its equal was not to be found. There was a demand for poteen at that time and a wedding without poteen was unheard of. West Clare was seldom without its share and whatever drop was left after the Christmas celebrations was soon swept away by wedding parties. But [sadly] sometimes there wasn't a drop to be got.[14]

The life of the poteen-maker was not an easy one. At all times he operated under difficult conditions, in isolated places, hounded by excise men and officers of the law, who could destroy his tools, empty his containers so that not a drop remained, and impose hefty fines. To make matters worse, his activities were frowned upon by the Church. In certain dioceses the making of poteen was a "reserved sin," which meant that only the local bishop had power to absolve the sinner. A story told in Erris, Co Mayo, contains the motif of an international folk tale. It goes:

> I saw stacks of worms and other poteen making equipment stacked outside Cornboy church during a mission [a series of evening devotions given by a visiting preacher and once held in every Catholic church during the season of Lent]. It was said that one man who was a good hand at making poteen went to a neighbour's house on his way to the mission, where he intended to confess his sins. He asked the woman of the house who was rocking a baby to take the child out of the cradle. He got into the cradle and asked the woman to rock him. He did this so he could quite literally tell the priest that he had not touched a drop of poteen since he was last rocked in a cradle...[The storyteller ended his tale with a fine boastful line.] I myself first tasted poteen when I was seven years old. We got a spoonful each in a neighbour's house. [15]

At one time almost every housewife made her own wine. The only essential additives to wine that is not meant to be stored and kept are yeast, sugar and water, and in many cases the methods used were of the simplest. The list of the most popular of the home brews included wine made from sloes, blackberries, elderberries, rhubarb, apple, cider, beetroot, cranberries, nettles; home-brewed wheat and potato wine; carrot wine, celery tea, dandelion tea, tansy tea, bogbean wine and ginger beer. Ale was made in many households up to fifty years ago. Lukewarm water in which treacle and brown sugar were added was poured into a bottle containing the ale plant seed and left for ten days, when it was ready for drinking. An account from Ardee, Co Louth, says:

> It was a wonderful sight to see the ale plant fermenting and
> the bubbles rising; every so often the spawn would have
> to be divided and thrown away. I have yet to taste ale like
> that which came from the ale plant. It could be made
> alcoholic by adding brandy and sugar. [16]

Many of the wines or fruit drinks were said to have curative powers. Dandelion tea, made from the roots or leaves of the dandelion and bottled, was said to be a cure for bed-wetting; mixed with whiskey and bottle it was also used by people with chest ailments. Cowslip wine was said to be good for the complexion. In Cork a tea made from boiling wild carrots was used for rheumatism. One of the most popular drinks all over the country was made from bogbean, known as the *báchrán* or *bahrams*. In Donegal they said, "Drink bahrams in March and nettles in Mye [May] and you'll not need a doctor till the day you die." Roots of the bogbean, which are white, run underground and have small stems. In the month of March it was usual to take up the roots and clean them in water. They were then boiled, and sugar was added to taste. It was a drink guaranteed to clear the blood.

Coffee, like tea, made a late appearance on the culinary scene in Ireland. The coffee houses of 18th-century Dublin were well-known places of rendezvous for the merchants and men of letters as well as fashionable beaux. Over the coffee pot the day's newspapers were read, gossip exchanged, and intrigues hatched. Widespread acceptance of coffee was slow, however, and well into our own times coffee was produced in many rural households only for the returned Yank or American visitor. It took the introduction of instant coffee and more venturesome palates to make it the popular drink it is today.

Tea was introduced to these islands in the early part of the 18th century, and, like coffee and chocolate, was first drunk by the wealthy and leisured. It took over a century for it to become part of the staple diet of the Irish people. A breakfast of tea and white bread was considered a luxury well into the middle of the 19th century and produced only for important visitors. In William Carleton's pre-famine story "Going to Maynooth" the obnoxious Denis O'Shaughnessy, conscious of his exalted status as a clerical student, announces to his unfortunate father,

> In future I'm resolved to have my "tay" breakfast every morning.[17]

Times were hard and tea was bought sparingly, if at all. In the manuscript material of the Department of Irish Folklore, an informant in Co Sligo recalls that long ago tea was only bought at Christmas. A half-ounce was used and the remainder kept over until Easter. The same was true of much of the country.

Stories are told of the confusion over methods of preparation that arose when tea was first introduced. In the Glens of Antrim they remember when a local man, a sailor, first brought a pound of tea home to his wife. The priest was invited in to enjoy this luxury, and the sailor's wife duly served the meal, setting down one plate of tea leaves in front of her husband and another in front of the reverend guest with the telling remark, "I don't begrudge you your taste." Much the same story is told in Wexford. "When tea first came to these parts they never used the liquid. After brewing, the liquid was thrown out and the leaves eaten spread on bread and with milk to drink."

Like many itinerant traders, the "tay" man was a familiar figure in the Irish countryside, going from house to house selling spills of tay. In the west of Ireland he is remembered best as *Seáinín a' tae*—Seán of the tea.

Drinking tea could be considered a waste and an extravagance and a cause of idleness. As late as 1945 they still remembered in the Glens of Antrim the days "when tea-drinking was looked on with disfavour. It wouldn't do for a girl to become known as a tea-drinker. It would go against her in marriage. The men were death on the women and their wives using it." And a cautionary tale:

This woman made a tin of tea and it was very hot. The men
came in without warning and she put the tin of hot tea
between her feet at the fire and pulled down her long skirts
over it. She didn't spill a drop or scald herself and said,
"God sent three angels out of the north to keep me safe."[18]

Tea was considered a luxury in many parts of Ireland in the 19th
century and was given to servant boys and labouring men on
Sundays and Church holidays as a special treat. In Kerry they
described what was commonplace in many parts:

All the payment a man might ask for jobs such as helping
with a litter of pigs, was a good fire, the tea can and a teapot
under his arm. Women who arrived to do such work as
plucking geese, cutting seed [i.e. for potato planting],
washing clothes, would refuse to stay unless they were
assured of the odd smoke and tea several times a day. The
tin can made by the local tinsmith with a handle on one
side made do for a teapot in many homes. The can or teapot
was seldom out of the *gríosach* or ashes and tea might be
brewed up to ten times a day. It wasn't considered worth
drinking unless it was so strong you could dance a mouse
on it. [19]

The tea on the draw, the ever-ready offer of a cup to a neighbour,
was a sign of hospitality. "Is it leave with the curse of the house
on you?" was said if a visitor refused food or drink. Bargaining
between a couple of men at a fair generally needed the help of a
go-between, who might say to the reluctant buyer, "Make the dale,
be a decent man. You come of good stock. Sure your mother never
took the teapot from the fire." Tea soon became such an addiction
with adults that a common saying was *Marbh le tae agus marbh gan
é*—dead from tea and dead without it. However, whether from
reasons of economy or health, children were seldom given tea
except at Christmas and Easter. Instead they drank milk or cocoa.

REFERENCES

1. James Carney, "The Impact of Christianity," in *Early Irish Society*, ed. Myles Dillon, Dublin, 1954, 143.
2. Fynes Moryson, *The Commonwealth of Ireland*, 1617.
3. The Four Masters. *The Annals of the Kingdom of Ireland*, ed. John O'Donovan, Dublin, 1845-51.
4. *Drinks of the World*, 1892, quoting *Delights for Ladies*, 1602, 21.
5. Fynes Moryson, *An Itinerary During His Ten Years' Travel*, 1617 (1907-08 ed.), 36.
6. Derricke, *The Image of Ireland*, 1581 (1883 ed.), 109.
7. Op. cit.
8. Constantia Maxwell, *Irish History from Contemporary Sources*, 1936, 320.
9. Carew, *Calendar of State Papers*, 1587-88.
10. George O'Brien, *Economic History of Ireland in the 17th Century*, London, 1919, 38-44.
11. Tomás de Bhaldraithe (ed. and trans.), *Cinnlae Amlaoibh*, Dublin,1970.
12. Dept of Folklore Questionnaire (Drinks).
13. Ib.
14. Ib.
15. Ib.
16. Ib.
17. William Carleton, . *Traits and Stories of the Irish Peasantry*, Dublin, 1830-33, 138.
18. Department of Irish Folklore, MS 1363, 123.
19. See n. 12.

4

The Lordly Salmon

"O Lord, make me a salmon that I may swim with the others through the clear green waters." This was the prayer of the maiden Lí Bhán or Muiraidhin (born of the sea), daughter of the high king Eochaidh. She alone of all her family survived when Lough Neagh overflowed its banks and the palace was submerged. She was fated to live in her *grianán*, or bower, under the lake, and when she saw the speckled fish swimming all around her she longed to be with them. Her prayers were answered, she was changed into a salmon and her lapdog into an otter, and they both lived three hundred years under the sea. In this ancient tale where pagan and Christian traditions are interwoven we find one of the earliest mentions of the salmon. Not alone was the salmon considered the most delicious of food but it was credited with having magical powers. To wish a person the health of the salmon was to wish them strength, agility and a long life. In Irish folk belief there is a mystical connection between the salmon and the life force. *Bradán beatha* was the life essence or soul, and *ór do bhradáin bheatha a chur amach* meant to die (as of shock or sorrow).

Salmon is mentioned time and again in the heroic tales of kings and chieftains. Cormac Mac Airt, the legendary king who reigned in Ireland in pre-Christian times, is said to have choked on the bone of a salmon. An earlier tale tells of the king's visit to *Tír Tairngire*, the Land of Promise, and his astonishment at the sight of an enchanted fountain full of magical salmon. The most famous salmon in Irish mythology is to be found in the story of Connla's Well, around which grew nine hazel trees which produced blossoms and nuts simultaneously. Whenever a nut fell into the water it was swallowed by a salmon, and for each nut swallowed a bright red spot appeared on the belly of the fish, which was known as the Salmon of Knowledge. In the Fionn tales this salmon again makes an appearance. As a young boy Fionn became a pupil of Finéigeas, the most famous poet in Ireland, who had made his home beside the river Boyne. On an evening when the fish were rising, Finéigeas crossed the greensward carrying a basket made of osiers in which lay a splendid salmon. "For seven years I have waited to catch this fish," he told Fionn, "Take it and cook it for my supper but on no account eat any of the flesh, for it was foretold that a poet would catch this salmon and that whoever had the first taste would have all knowledge." "I shall not eat the tiniest bit," the boy promised earnestly, and put the salmon down to roast on a fire of apple wood. The delicious smell would have tempted the gods themselves, let alone a hungry boy, but Fionn had given his word. He would cook the salmon to perfection and serve it with fresh cress and crusty bread, and then afterwards they would both drink a cup of mead to celebrate. He watched anxiously as the fish turned a golden brown and pressed with his thumb a blister which rose on the skin. Because he had burnt his thumb he popped it into his mouth to relieve the pain and so unwittingly had the first taste of the salmon and became the wisest of men. He knew at once that something magical had happened to him and was frightened at what Finéigeas would say, but the poet was wise and knew that no one can escape his fate. Ever after, if Fionn wished to look into the future or to find the answer to a question that puzzled the world, he had only to suck on his thumb and all was revealed.

Fish played a large part in the diet of the early monks, ascetic men who mortified their flesh by a spartan diet of watercress and barley bread and who might allow themselves a meal of honey or fish on the Sabbath or a feast day. Now it is good manners to eat whatever is served up at table, more especially if one is a guest, but the early saints were stern men who did not believe in bending rules. On one occasion St Molua, who had killed a fatted calf for St Maedoc, was chagrined to discover that his guest refused to eat meat. However, miracles were commonplace in those far-off days. In an instant Molua had changed the flesh meat into fish. Much the same story is told of St Ciarán, who changed a gammon of bacon into bread, fish and honey to feed one of the brethren. Yet another story tells of how when Colm Cille and his monks came to seek the hospitality of St Comhghall at Bangor the power of the Lord caused great shoals of fish to swim up to the walls of the monastery, where they were easily caught in nets so that there was full and plenty for all.

Still more wonderful are the stories of fish gathered on dry land. Lupita, the sister of St Patrick, shared the same dwelling as the saintly Bishop Mel, as was the custom in the early church with men and women under vows. Slanderous gossip was spread around by some ill-intentioned person that the pair were united in more than prayer. To prove his innocence the bishop ploughed a field behind his house, out of which he netted many fish both large and small, while Lupita carried hot coals in her gown and neither her person nor the habit she wore was even scorched. After this, we are told, monks and nuns thought it prudent to live in separate dwellings. Not only does the story show that fish formed part of the early diet but it proves that scandal-mongers are to be found in every age.

In the mid-17th century Dr Massari commented on the oysters in our waters, of huge size and in such abundance that none better could be desired. He wrote:

> The fish of both river and sea are so exquisite and so abundant that the common people have pike, hake, salmon, trout, indeed all sorts of fish and these are to be had for astonishing value. We bought pilchard and oysters very cheaply indeed.[1]

Fish, including pilchards and herrings, was eaten in quantities in the 17th and 18th centuries. Herrings were known as the food

of the poor and, indeed, they saved many from hunger. Great shoals
were regularly seen off the Donegal coast, and Malahide on the
outskirts of Dublin was noted for its herring fleet. Jonathan Swift,
Dean of St Patrick's in the Liberties of Dublin evoked the street cries
of the 18th-century fishmongers in his verse:

Be not sparing,
Leave off swearing,
Buy my herrings
Fresh from Malahide,
Better was never tried.
Come eat 'em with pure fresh butter and mustard,
Their bellies are soft, and as white as custard.
Come, sixpence a dozen to get me some bread,
Or like my own herrings, I too shall be dead.[2]

In 1748, at the end of a year of near-famine, herrings relieved
want dramatically. Five years later an unnamed traveller wrote an
account of his travels in the Rosses, Co Donegal, and commented
on how important a part fish played in the diet of the common
people.

Their usual summer diet consists of milk, curds, butter,
with most excellent fish of several kinds. In winter they live
on potatoes, fish, rabbits, butter and a little bread made of
barley or oaten meal. In one of the largest islands, called
Oiey [Owey], they used kill a great number of seals which
they salted for winter and were so fond of it as to prefer
it to any other kind of meat.[3]

This custom of eating seal meat is unusual. Generally there was
a taboo against eating seals because of the belief that members of
certain families could change themselves or be changed into seals.
Fish was eaten not only along the coast but up to thirty miles
inland. Amhlaoibh Ó Súilleabháin, the Kilkenny diarist of the 1820s,
who was something of a gourmet, ate only fresh fish. He noted:

I do not like salt fish and fresh fish was not to be had except
too dear and too seldom.[4]

Fresh hake, sole, turbot and of course salmon were all to be
found on the tables of the prosperous merchants and landowners.
The common people ate cod, haddock, whiting, mackerel and
herring, pike, perch and eel. Yet though we were well provided
with a variety of sea and freshwater fish, many households, more
especially inland, seldom if ever ate fresh fish. Dried whiting, ling
and rock cod hung from the kitchen rafters of the small cabin or
the prosperous farmhouse, and fish both dried and salted could be
bought in small country shops that sold everything from bootlaces
to home-cured ham. Indeed dried fish often provided the only
condiment to the potato when times were bad. The old saying, "Dip
in the dip and leave the herring for your father," shows the shifts
to which the poverty-stricken housewife of the 19th century was
put to feed her family, but it also proves how flavoursome potatoes
could taste with herring dip.

Fish ponds were in use from at least medieval times. Eel weirs
have a long history. From early on they appear to have been the
property of individual families, as were the nets. One legend tells
that certain fishermen, who either fished or owned the weirs,
refused fish to St Cainneach and his monks, and miraculously the
saint's *baculum* (crozier) was used for the catch.[5] . In a charming
story of the O'Brien family, who lived on the shores of Lough Gur,
Co Limerick, in the 19th century, Cissie, the daughter, describes
how the farm boasted an eel weir. Eels were sent direct to the
Limerick market, or taken by Meggy the Eel, an itinerant vendor
who came from Bruff to buy the take which she peddled from house
to house.[6]

Almost seventy years later an equally delightful story was
written of life on the edge of the great Bog of Allen in the 1920s
as remembered by Maura Laverty. She says:

Living so far inland our fish dishes were mostly ling or red
herrings. Occasionally, however, Mike Brophy took his

fishing rod and went down to the mill pond returning with
a few eels or perch. Judy Ryan [the servant girl] would
never touch an eel, saying that they were cousins to the
serpents. Eels could be fried...A favourite method of cooking
eels was to skin the fish, cut them in slices, set them to
parboil to take out the grease, then stew them in a creamy
white sauce with chopped parsley and scallions.[7]

An amusing legend common to Ireland and the Scottish Isles
is told about the flounder. St Colm Cille was out in a boat one day
when he noticed a shoal of flounders passing by. "Is this a removal,
flounder?" the saint asked a pert fish that had stuck up its head.
"Yes it is, crooked legs," retorted the cheeky fish. "If I have crooked
legs may you have a crooked mouth," came the malediction from
the sorely tried saint; and so it is to this day that the flounder has
a wry mouth.

Mounds of shells have been discovered in archaeological digs,
especially around the western seaboard. Some of these denote early
dye factories: certain shellfish were used to produce the costly
purple dyestuffs beloved of kings and princes but mostly they
represent the remains of food once eaten. Shellfish was always a
popular food; indeed it was noted that the palate of the common
folk far exceeded that of the gentry for lobsters and crustaceans of
every kind. During the famine years many people, homeless and
starving, wandered the coastline in search of cockles, winkles, birds'
eggs, seaweed—anything to assuage the hunger pangs. This,
coupled with the fact that the eating of contaminated fish had been
a common cause of death, persisted in folk memory and turned
people against shellfish. It has taken over a century to change this
prejudice.

Shellfish formed part of the diet of medieval Dublin, as is
evident from the remains found in the Viking excavation in the
High Street, and the tradition lived on up to our own times. The
cockle and periwinkle woman who sold her wares in the Liberties
of Dublin, measuring out the fish by the cup from a tin basin, was
a common sight in Francis Street, New Street, Patrick Street and

around Christ Church.

Sandymount Strand was the favourite cockle ground of the citizens of Dublin until the waters of Dublin Bay became polluted in recent years. It was a common sight during the summer months to see crowds of Dublin women and children picking cockles when the tide was out. The experienced cockle picker knew the special markings on the strand: where the sand curled like a worm was the place to dig. The fish could be extracted from the shell with a pin and eaten on the spot, but cockles were usually taken home, where they were well washed to remove the sand and then boiled. They were a favourite Dublin supper dish.

Fisherfolk had a saying that cockles could not be eaten until they had three drinks of April water. The tide had to come in three times, then the season for cockle picking started. Leo Corduff, a folklore collector for the Department of Irish Folklore, remembers: "In Rossport, Co Mayo, we also picked barnachs (limpets) and periwinkles, mussels and bandals, which were like large mussels, and could be got in thousands like the cockle, but you had to dig them up with a spade." In the north of the country *duileasc* or dulse (a reddish-brown seaweed which could be eaten raw or boiled in soup) has always been popular. At the Lammas Fair in Ballycastle, Co Antrim, dulse and yallaman (yellowman: home-made golden-yellow toffee) sold at stalls were traditionally given by a boy to his sweetheart:

> At the auld Lammas Fair, were you ever there?
> Were you ever at the fair of Ballycastle, oh?
> Did you treat your Mary Anne to dulse and yallaman
> At the auld Lammas Fair of Ballycastle, oh?

Carrageen moss, found on the rock at low tide, was much used along the coast. Boiled in milk it made delicious jellies and blancmanges. It was said to be very nutritious and a folk cure for colds and chest ailments, as it contained iron. In lean times in Donegal the freshly gathered carrageen was washed and boiled in water and given to calves to supplement their food.

The western seaboard has always been noted for the richness of the catch, none more so than Galway Bay, the most famous fishing ground in Ireland, and for a long time traditionally the exclusive property of a community of fishermen who lived in a settlement near the Spanish Arch, known as the *Cladach* (Claddagh) or Beach.

The community, which flourished up to the end of the 1940s, dated from an early period when it was said the tribes of Galway, proud of their kingly descent, refused to mix with the neighbouring population. The people of the Claddagh lived in thatched cottages with walls of great thickness, or in black beehive huts whose architectural style goes back to early Christian Ireland. The remains of such beehive huts can still be seen on the Dingle Peninsula in Co Kerry. The community had its own dialect and elected its own mayor or king, whose laws were implicitly obeyed.

Strangers or "transplanters" were not welcomed, and the people married within the community. The wedding, or Claddagh, ring, as it was known, was made of thick gold embossed with the emblem of two hands entwined, and was handed down from mother to daughter. These fisherfolk were fiercely independent and stubbornly obeyed certain rules and observed certain superstitions relating to the sea.

When the potato failed, fishermen all over Ireland pawned or sold their gear to buy meal. Still strong in folk memory is the tragedy of fishermen of the Claddagh in Galway and those around Achill, Belmullet and Killybegs, selling their tackles, nets and boats when the crop failed in 1845 to buy seed potatoes and meal, little dreaming that the terrible famine would last all of three years.

The Society of Friends (or Quakers, as they are popularly known) have always been one of the most respected religious sects in Ireland. During the years of the great hunger of 1845–47, they worked ceaselessly to feed the starving and nurse the dying. Even when everyone else had given up in despair they laboured on. When in June 1849 they were finally forced to abandon relief work, Ireland lost some of its most faithful friends.

During the famine years they were asked by the government of the day to help the Claddagh fishermen, who were starving within sight of seas teeming with fish because they had neither nets nor boats. But even the gentle and selfless Quakers were exasperated by some of the setbacks they encountered. "The people of the Claddagh are incorrigible," the Quakers reported, "and some of their laws should be broken. They will only take boats out fishing on certain days and at certain times, and if other boats go out, so outraged are they at the flaunting of their superstitions that they will attack the crews."

However, with all their faults they were a strongly individualistic people, and the fact that the Claddagh is no more has left Galway that much less colourful. Stubborn and tenacious they may have been, but these are qualities that are most needed by fisherfolk.

It is probably true to say that generosity is most marked amongst the poor and underprivileged, and this is as true for Dublin's inner city as for a remote hamlet on the western seaboard. Fisherfolk were always noted for open-handedness amongst their own. In an account from Henry Morris we read:

> The ordinary crew of a fishing boat in Tir Chonaill during the first half of the last century was eight. But when the boat returned the catch was divided not into eight parts but into ten equal divisions. One for the upkeep of the boat, and one for the widows and orphans who had no one to fish for them. This very Christian practice is no longer observed.[8]

Men who go down to the sea in boats have always been noted for courage, and this is especially true of the fishermen who braved the stormy elements in their frail curachs, with little between them and a watery grave but the grace of God and a stretching of canvas and skin over wood. Peig Sayers, who lived all her married life in the Great Blasket Island, in her book *Machnamh Sean-Mhná—An Old Woman's Reflections*—looks out on the tranquil sea and recalls the calm morning when as a girl she saw three boats set out from the mainland of Dunquin opposite the Blaskets. There were eight men in each boat, including her father and two brothers. She remembers how on the return journey a rough tidal wave put them in danger so that one of the boats sank. "It was a sorrowful day in Dunquin," she says, "There were five widows and their orphans weeping bitterly."[9]

The same theme is found in John Millington Synge's evocative play *Riders to the Sea*. The scene is set on an island off the west coast of Ireland. Maurya, the old woman, has lost her husband, her father-in-law and her six sons to the sea, and with the heartbreaking patience that such woman have forged, she echoes the lament of every wife and mother of a drowned fisherman:

> They're all together this time and the end has come...
> Michael has a clean burial in the far north by the grace of
> the Almighty God. Bartley will have a fine coffin out of the
> white boards and a deep grave surely. What more can we
> want than that? No man at all can be living for ever, and
> we must be satisfied.[10]

REFERENCES

1. Kavanagh, op.cit.
2. From "Verses Made for the Women Who Cry Apples & c." (1746).
3. In Joseph C. Walker, *Memoir of the Armour and Weapons of the Irish*, Dublin, 1758.
4. Tomás de Bhaldraithe, op. cit.
5. Plummer (trans.), *Vitae Sanctorum Hiberniae, I*.
6. Mary Carbery, *The Farm by Lough Gur*, London, 1938, 20.
7. Maura Laverty, *Never No More*, London, 1942, 31.
8. *Béaloideas* IX, 1939.
9. Peig Sayers, *Machnamh Sean-Mhná*, London, 1962, 1.
10. J M Synge, *Riders to the Sea*, 1904.

5

The Dun Cow

Irish beef, veal, lamb, fresh pork and bacon have always been noted for their excellence and eaten in considerable quantities from earliest times right down to the 20th century. Undoubtedly the consumption of meat increased with the change in food patterns, together with improvement in animal foodstuffs and the introduction of new techniques of freezing and curing meat in the late 19th and 20th centuries. Earlier on, milk foods and grain—oats, barley, rye—buttressed the diet during the summer months. At the approach of winter it was usual to drive cattle down from their summer pastures to be slaughtered and eaten. Surplus meat was salted and hung to be used during the lean months of winter and early spring.

Cattle might be bred for the milk they gave; sheep were important for the wool they provided; but the only reason for pig-rearing was as a source of food. The introduction of the potato to Ireland in Elizabethan times and its widespread adoption in the centuries that followed meant that in good years even the meanest hovel could afford to rear a pig, for the animal could be fed on surplus potatoes and potato skins. Up to late medieval times, when the land was heavily wooded, domestic pigs were fattened on mast: the fruit of the beech, oak, chestnut or whitethorn. This food was said to give the flesh of the swine a delicious flavour and was so enjoyed by them that they would travel great distances did they get but the scent. In the early literature, it is related that a certain oakwood was to be found on the western part of the plain of Macha and that

> no mast was ever like its mast for size and for fragrance.
> When the wind would blow over it, the odour thereof
> would be smelt throughout Erin, to what point soever the
> wind would carry the scent so that it was a heartbreak to
> the swine of Ireland when it reached them.[1]

One of the finest of the king sagas is *The Destruction of Da Derga's Hostel*, preserved in the *Book of the Dun Cow*. The story is set in the reign of Conaire the Great, who had his court at Tara some time before the rise of Niall of the Nine Hostages. Da Derga's Hostel was one of the principal houses of hospitality and was situated at Bohernabreena—the road of the hostel—at the foot of the Dublin mountains. Now in Conaire's reign there were three crowns of plenty on the land: fish in every river and lake, ships laden with goods at every port and oak mast up to the knees in autumn to fatten the pigs. Because of his connection with the *Tuatha Dé Danann* or fairy people the king was bound by certain *geasa* or taboos. He should not spend more than nine nights away from Tara, he should not go right hand wise round Tara nor left hand wise round Mag Breg, and three Reds should not go before him into the house of a red-haired man. But even the wisest ruler can err, and on a visit to Da Derga's Hostel the king broke his taboos with disastrous results. Mauraders attacked and set fire to the hostel, and the river Dodder, which ran through the great hall, dried up.

And so died King Conaire. Outside there was no moon: the sky was not dark but slashed with crimson flames like a great river of blood. Then the walls fell down and thus was accomplished the destruction of Da Derga's Hostel. Famine and rapine followed and oak mast was found in the land no more.

The Dun Cow which belonged to St Ciarán of Clonmacnoise is the most famous cow in the literature. In the earliest life of the saint (written down around 1100) it was related that Ciarán as a young boy left home to study under St Finian so that he might read the

Scripture. He asked his parents for a parting gift of a cow which would provide him with milk while at school. At first he was refused, his mother giving the excuse that "the other little boys do not have cows." However, according to legend, Ciarán was wise beyond his years and, trusting that a miracle would take place, blessed the prize cow of the herd when crossing his father's meadow; whereupon the cow followed him on his way. His parents, taking this as a sign, gave him the animal as a gift. The story goes that not only the cow but also its calf followed Ciarán. When he reached Clonard, on the borders of Leinster and Uí Néill, he marked out a grazing ground with his staff between cow and calf. Beyond this mark the calf could not go, though the cow could lick her young across the divide. *Odhar Chiaráin*—Ciarán's Dun Cow— "supplied an incredible amount of milk each day, sufficient to divide amongst a multitude and to feed every pupil at the school..."and to this day, the *Life* continues, "the hide of the Dun Cow is most honoured in the city of Clonmacnoise, and any disciple of St Ciarán who by the grace of God dies on this skin will possess eternal life."[1]

The tradition is that *Leabhar na hUidhre*—the Book of the Dun Cow—was written on the vellum or hide of Ciarán's cow. The manuscript contains the great compilation of early Irish secular literature and was written down at Clonmacnoise before 1106.

So important was mast crop in animal husbandry that the *Annals of Innisfallen*, the *Annals of Ulster* and the *Annals of the Kingdom of Ireland* record bumper yields on hundreds of occasions between the years 576 and 1310. So abundant was the mast, we are told, that undersized piglets were fattened, and healthy pigs grew great. The right to pasture pigs in woods, called *pannage*, was an integral part of Anglo-Norman economy and was included in agreements between overlords and their tenants. Mention is made of this custom in the registers of religious houses of the period, while it is commonplace in documents of the 14th and 15th centuries in the *Red Book of Ossory*.[3]

Deer were plentiful in early Ireland and were valued for food, hide and horns, and were even kept as pets. In the stories of Fionn and the Fianna we read of hunters chasing the deer and feasting on venison as well as the flesh of the wild boar. According to the *Book of Rights*, the prerogative of the king of Ireland in early times was to receive a tribute of venison. Badgers, too, were eaten in early times. The story of the tragic Deirdre is contained in the epic *Táin Bó Cuailgne*—the Cattle Raid of Cooley. Deirdre fled to Scotland with her lover, Naoise, and his two brothers, and when these sons of Uisneach were lured back to Ireland by the high king, who wished to marry Deirdre, and were treacherously slain, she wept over their graves, recalling the fine times they knew in Scotland and remembering how the sons of Uisneach brought her food, fish and venison and the flesh of the badger.

Tributes were paid in kine: the king of Leinster sent his Munster overlord a hundred of every kind of cattle, while church tithes of the first fruits included the first calf or first-born male of every milk-bearing animal. According to legend, when Aodh Dubh, King of Breifne, reputed to be the ugliest man in Ireland, was baptised by Saint Maedoc, the king besought the saint to work a miracle to enhance his looks. Maedoc wrapped the king's head in a monk's cowl, and when the ceremony was over and the cowl thrown back, Aodh Dubh—Black Hugh—was so changed that ever after he was called Aodh Fionn—Fair Hugh. He gave the saint as tribute a cow from every stead, an ox from every raid, a foal from every stud, a pig from every sty, a sheep from every flock, and a stable of horses.

Cattle were used in payment or barter. In the Brehon Laws it was laid down that a tenant should pay his overlord two cows with their accompaniments as rent, while the payment due to the Culdee monks was a milch-cow if a student they had tutored could recite the Psalter, hymns, and canticles. For a year's tuition, with bed and board the charge was a calf, several hogs, three sacks of malt and a sack of corn.

In earlier times goat meat was eaten, but the animals were mainly kept for the nutritious milk they provided and for the cheeses made from the milk. However, except in mountainous and rocky regions, the natural habitat of the goat, it became more profitable to breed sheep and oxen. The old Irish goat was small,

sometimes white in colour but more generally iron-grey. Making
a bargain in Connacht it was usual to swear by all the goats in
Connemara.

Goat's flesh is occasionally mentioned in the early records as a
food, though probably it meant the flesh of the kid. The tradition
of eating young goat lingered on in Kerry even when it had died
out in other parts of the country. An account recorded in the 1940s
by a folklorist tells how people managed in earlier times when food
was scarce:

> They hadn't any tea then, but potatoes three times a day,
> and fish and a little meat now and again. The people of the
> glens had plenty of meat because they kept goats, but some
> had only little holdings. Some people might not taste meat
> from one Christmas day to the next.[4]

At the beginning of the 17th century, Fynes Moryson remarked
on the great quantities of unsalted beef and swine that the ordinary
person devoured and the fact that they seldom ate mutton.[5]

This fact is noted time and again by observers in the centuries
that followed. As we know, even on the eve of the Great Famine
servants and farm workers on substantial holdings might be fed
meat three times a week. It is sometimes difficult to know whether
the spartan diet of milk, potatoes and fish consumed regularly by
tenant farmers and their like was the the result of poverty or the
fear of appearing prosperous. In the manuscript material of the
Department of Irish Folklore we find the following item from south
of the Nagles Mountains in Co Cork relating to food supply in the
19th century:

> Of necessity the farmer had to keep a poor table lest the
> landlord or his agent would know that he was well-to-do.
> If this was known the farmer would pay dearly for it, his
> rent would be put up for next gale day, or a portion of his
> farm would be given to some well wisher of the landlord.
> Resisting this wrong he would kill a beef at Christmas and
> Easter and share with his poor neighbours.[6]

It is interesting to note that, however hard the times, horse-meat was never eaten. It was considered taboo.

Down the centuries, whether in times of prosperity or near-famine, whenever a farmer killed a bullock, a sheep or a pig, he would "share the killing" with all those less fortunate. Traditionally, special portions were given to the smith working the forge, to the local nurse or midwife and to the priest of the parish.

While Irish beef has always been noted for its flavour, corned beef was equally relished. Boiled and served with green cabbage and floury potatoes, it was considered an epicurean dish, to be eaten at Hallowe'en, at Christmas, on St Patrick's Day, at weddings and at wakes, a tradition that was carried to the New World by the emigrants of the 18th and 19th centuries. To this day, corned beef and cabbage are served on St Patrick's Day and at Thanksgiving in parts of North America.

Bacon, corned beef, sausages and puddings are all mentioned in *The Vision of Mac Conglinne*, the 12th-century tale that also describes the condiments served with meats. Mac Conglinne, in an attempt to coax the demon of gluttony out of the king's belly, orders Pichan, a wealthy chieftain, to provide him with "juicy old bacon, tender corned beef, a side of mutton, a comb of honey, English salt on a silver dish and four perfectly straight hazel spits to carry the joints." When these are provided, Mac Conglinne ties a linen apron around his middle, puts a linen cap on his head, lights a fire of clean ash wood and proceeds to cook portions of meat on white hazel spits. "As the meat splatters and sizzles he busies himself rubbing salt and honey into one piece after another with the speed of a deer or a swallow, or a bare spring wind in March."

Spring lamb of a melting tenderness flavoured with rosemary, garlic or other herbs was considered a great Irish dish. Mutton was boiled, roasted, used in pies and stewed. During a recording session in Holyoke, Massachusetts, some years ago, Dr Séamas Ó Catháin, Archivist of the Department of Irish Folklore, met a Kerry-born woman who had spent most of her adult life in America but who still remembered the delicious mutton pies of her youth, made in her home on the Dingle Peninsula. The pies were baked in a pot-oven or cooker, then the top crust was broken and the pies dropped into the mutton broth made with the bones and vegetables. They were a speciality of the district.

Irish stew, famous the world over, is a peasant dish that originated in the small Irish cottage or cabin where cooking utensils were scarce and where meat and vegetables could all be cooked in one pot. Similar methods of cooking were used in the industrial regions of the north of England. Lancashire hotpot, still a regional favourite, was made in a similar manner to Irish stew, cooked in a large earthenware or iron pot or stewpan. In the mining districts of south Wales it was customary to cook meat, cabbage, potatoes and any other vegetables in a type of tiered oven or large pot with separate sections.

Traditionally Irish stew was made with mutton chops trimmed of fat, potatoes, onions, carrots, chopped parsley and water or stock, cooked over a slow heat and thickened with potatoes. It was one of the great Irish dishes guaranteed to put a "heart in a person and counteract the winter's cold." Irish stew made with spare ribs and griskins at pig-killing time was considered even more tasty.

Most households killed a pig at certain times of the year, and in the more substantial farms several pigs were usually killed on the same day. Certain superstitions were once observed regarding the time of killing. A pig should never be killed unless there was a letter R in the month, which meant in effect that pigs were seldom slaughtered during the summer months. In the counties of Mayo and Galway it was believed that the killing should take place under a full moon. If the animal was killed when the moon was waning the meat would reduce in size, while if the killing was done when the moon was waxing or full the meat would increase. [7]

Killing the pig was an important social occasion, for it meant full and plenty for all. Each neighbour who came to help with the pig killing brought a handful of salt for the curing, and when the work was done each would get a share of the puddings and the fresh pork. The slaughtering of the animal was done by the men, but it was the women who were responsible for curing and smoking the hams and bacon; these were particularly delicious if cured in the smoke of green wood. When the pig was killed the blood was collected in a vessel and used to make black puddings. In Ring, Co Waterford, they described the old method used:

> Long ago when they killed pigs they kept the intestines to make puddings. They washed them clear in a running stream and they were left to soak in spring water overnight. The casings were cut into fifteen inch lengths, tied at one end. Salt, lard, oatmeal, finely chopped onions, spices, peppers and cloves, together with a cup of flour were mixed with the pig's blood which had been collected in a bucket. Each pudding was three-quarters filled and tied at the end. It was dropped into a pot half-filled with water which had been brought to simmering point, cooked for about an hour, then taken up, allowed to cool, and divided amongst the neighbours. This was always done. When needed for use puddings were fried in a pan.[8]

White puddings were made in a similar manner but the blood was omitted. Toasted oatmeal, onions boiled and chopped finely, chopped lard, pepper and salt were favourite fillings. Black puddings made with sheep's blood called *drisheens* have long been traditional in Co Cork. In some places drisheen was also used to describe the black pudding made with pig's blood. An old man who worked as a farm labourer in Co Clare gives this account:

> The woman of the house put down the puddings to boil and you never tasted the like, they were so delicious. She put the liver and lights and heart in a pan to roast. Every single person who helped in the salting was given some of the pork to take home with them. The puddings were called drisheens. I spent some time working on a farm in Co Clare. Strong farmers they were and they had three daughters. They would kill three pigs and make drisheens for my breakfast. It wasn't right to kill a sow in young [carrying a litter]. If you did so there wouldn't be any good in the flesh.[9]

Pig-killing was a busy time for the farmer's wife. Not only were hams home-cured, and smoked, mouth-watering black and white puddings made, lard melted down, trimmings and spare ribs and griskins put aside for the stew, pork fillets fried or roasted, but every farmer's wife had a special way of dealing with brawn or collared heads. Some liked their brawn well salted, and the head and feet would be left overnight in a pickling crock. The head was boiled to a jelly, the meat taken off, chopped very small, then flavoured with pepper, allspice and finely ground nutmeg. This was put in a bowl or a mould with a little of the liquid, covered with a firm lid or a plate with a weight on top and left to set. When it was firm and turned out it was said to be a dish fit for a king.

Irish home-cured hams and bacon were generally regarded as the best in the world, but there was a fall in the consumption of home-cured bacon in the second half of the 19th century as bacon factories opened up in the main dairying regions of the country with a consequent rise in the export trade. In many cases Irish bacon was replaced by cheap, fat, imported American bacon which was a poor substitute, and which, with the widespread use of white bread and tea, had a deleterious effect on Irish diet. It is interesting to note Synge's observation on the eating habits of the people of the Aran Islands in the early years of the present century.

> They used no animal food except a little bacon and salt. The old woman says she would be very ill if she ate fresh meat. Some years before, tea, sugar and flour had come into general use. Salt fish was much more the staple diet than at present and I am told skin diseases were very common, though now rare on the islands.[10]

With improved standards of living in the 20th century, the consumption of home produced meat—beef, lamb, mutton, pork, bacon and ham—has risen dramatically. Most Irishmen (if not Irishwomen) are generally conservative eaters. A cooked Irish breakfast means bacon, egg, sausages and puddings served with wholemeal or toasted bread and tea or coffee; a satisfying main meal must contain meat, either roasted, grilled or boiled, with potatoes and one other vegetable, while high tea or supper means bacon, eggs, cold ham and salad or cold roast beef.

"Dublin Coddle," said to have been introduced by the Vikings who founded the city, was always a favourite Saturday-night Liberties dish. Made with smoked streaky bacon cut in cubes, pork sausages and Spanish onions, the mixture is covered with water, brought to the boil and cooked in a heavy saucepan over a low heat. Sliced raw potatoes are sometimes added to the cooking, but most Dubliners preferred the traditional variety, served with bread to mop up the gravy and meat, and washed down with hot strong tea.

REFERENCES

1. *Revue Celtique* 16, 1859, 54.
2. Plummer, "Life of St Ciarán of Clonmacnoise."
3. AT Lucas, "Irish Food before the Potato," *Gwerin*, III, 1960, 1-36.
4. Department of Irish Folklore, MS 146.
5. Derricke, op.cit.
6. Department of Irish Folklore, MS 1071, 137.
7. Ib., MS 433, 127; MS 1862, 142.
8. Ib., MS 1862, 113.
9. Ib., Mss. 444, 92.
10. JM Synge, *The Aran Islands*, 1907, 258.

6

The Icelandic Sagas

In the early sagas we find mouth-watering descriptions of great feasts at which the company quaffed enormous draughts of ale, mead and wine, ate beef from cattle reared on herbs, meadow hay and corn, boar fattened on fresh milk and fine meal, curds, wheat, kernels of nuts and beef broth. Such accounts would suggest that beef, fresh pork, bacon and venison formed the bulk of the diet of the ordinary person. The sober truth is that while the country's prosperity depended on cattle, while a man's wealth was judged on the extent of his herds and chieftains and princes engaged in cattle-raids to bolster their power and prestige, most people depended on corn and milk for their basic needs. That is not to say that their food lacked variety, especially during the summer or autumn months when growth was at its abundant best, but, like the potato of a later time, wheat, oats, barley and rye, used as bread or porridge, were the mainstay of many.

Freshly ground oatmeal mixed with butter often served as iron rations to soldiers on active service and was also part of food rents in the 16th and 17th centuries. This butter and oatmeal mixture, sometimes called *meanadhach* (the name is also applied to watery gruel), is mentioned as part of the fare given to the Culdee monks in the 9th century Rule of Tallaght. Their abbot, Maolruáin, laid down that "if a festival happened to fall on certain days the monks were given leave to make a gruel of meal and water."

Edmund Campion in his 16th-century *History of Ireland* writes:

> Oatmeal and butter they crame together.
> They drink whey milk and beef broth.
> Flesh they devour without bread.
> They swill in aqua vitae in quarts and pottles.

This food is mentioned again in an Icelandic saga of the 9th century and gives us a glimpse of life in those far-off days when Viking pirates raided our shores and the long-prowed ship meant death and disaster. These Vikings struck swiftly—this was the key to their success—carrying off what they could of gold plate, jewels and priceless manuscripts and taking boys and young men as galley slaves. We know little of what happened their captives, except for the occasional reference in a saga to some Irish custom, a legend remembered, or an anecdote such as how on one raid they ran short of water and their unhappy captives tried to help.

> Ingolfr landed in the place that is now called Ingolfshodfi (Ingolfr's Head), but Hjorleifr was wind-driven to the west. He got a shortage of water. Then the Irish thralls found the expedient of kneading meal and butter and said it would quench the thirst. They called it minabak. But when it was ready there was heavy rain and they collected water in the tents. And when the minabak started to become mouldy they threw it overboard and it came ashore in the place that is now called Minabakserr.[1]

Porridge, one of the oldest traditional foods, was taken for breakfast and supper, and could be made from wheat, oats or barley, cooked in water or milk, taken with cream, fresh milk, sour milk or buttermilk and flavoured with salt, butter or honey and, in later times, sugar. Of all the cereals wheat was the most highly regarded, whether used as bread or porridge, and is sometimes described as the food of kings and princes. In the *Senchus Mór*, the law relating to fosterage lays down the kinds and amounts of porridge to be given to children of different classes fostered out in early Ireland.

> The children of inferior grades are to be fed on porridge
> or stirabout made of oatmeal on buttermilk or water taken
> with stale butter and are to be given a bare sufficiency; the
> sons of chieftains are to be fed to satiety on porridge made
> of barley meal upon new milk, taken with fresh butter,
> while the sons of kings and princes are to be fed on
> porridge made of wheaten meal, upon new milk, taken
> with honey.[2]

Oliver Twist asking for more was no 19th-century invention. Even during Ireland's so-called "golden age" it would appear that the workhouse mentality prevailed where the children of the poor were concerned.

Porridge continued to be a favourite food. In Mac Conglinne's 12th-century *Vision* he dreams of "fair white porridge made of sheep's milk" and of "porridge the treasure that is smoothest and sweetest of all." Even after the general adoption of the potato in the 18th and 19th centuries, porridge or stirabout continued to be used as a breakfast food in town and country (except in the very poorest households, where potatoes were consumed three times daily).

While bacon and eggs as a breakfast dish became popular with the middle classes in the latter half of the 19th century, porridge was still eaten as a first course and always given to children and servants. In the comfortable O'Brien farm at Lough Gur in the Shannon region, we read that the three young daughters of the house, as well as the maids, were given porridge for breakfast, while the master and mistress ate boiled eggs. In the great houses of the Anglo-Irish ascendancy, where breakfast was a feast in itself, amongst the many silver dishes on the sideboard holding fish, venison pasty, ham and eggs, a pot of porridge was often found.

Breakfast cereals as we know them today are nothing new. In addition to oatmeal porridge various corn and meal mixtures were eaten and drunk. Whole hulled wheat boiled in milk was popular, as was raw oatmeal eaten with thick milk or cream or buttermilk.

Sowans, made from the shells or husks of oats, was widely used as a drink. The husks or chaffs (the residue left after the oatmeal was ground in the mill) were steeped in either hot or cold water for anything from four days to three weeks. Much depended on the season and the degree of acidity required. When fermentation was complete the mixture was sieved and the semi-white liquid, known as bull's milk, could be used as a substitute for milk in tea or for buttermilk when making bread. Bull's milk was taken on days of black fast, Spy Wednesday or Good Friday in Lent, and was considered a good drink for thirsty men on a hot day engaged in heavy work such as mowing grass with a scythe, cutting turf, or gathering in the harvest.

Flummery was another oatmeal dish made by cooking the strained oatmeal liquid over the fire. It was brought to the boil and stirred briskly until it thickened to the consistency of a blancmange. If sugar and whipped cream were added to the oatmeal jelly it made a delicious confection. In the Glens of Antrim it was believed that there was a love charm in sowans. "If you stirred it in a certain way and then gave the liquid to your boy to drink you had him hooked." Many and varied were the sayings about sowans. In Co Mayo, a stupid person was said to be "as thick as flummery," while in Co Antrim the promise "I'll pay you daycintly with meal and seeds," meant you'd get no payment at all. In Fermanagh they said, "Bleed you for a cold and feed you on sowans," "Sowans in the porridge on a hill would run a mill," and "Sowans stirred anti-clockwise when boiling, you couldn't do that. You might as well try to sup sowans with a knitting needle."

REFERENCES

1. *Landnamabok*, I-III, 1900.
2. *Ancient Laws of Ireland*, Vol. 2 (on different kinds of food suitable for different social grades of children in fosterage), 148-151.

7

The Cake Dance

"Bread is older than man," says the Hungarian proverb, which is something of an overstatement. However, there is no doubt that bread is one of the earliest foods used by man. While prehistoric man set out from his cave to hunt and shoot, snare and trap animals, fish and birds, his womenfolk crushed simple grains which were mixed to a crude dough and cooked on a hot stone, under the ashes of the fire or in a makeshift oven—methods of baking which were used in many an Irish kitchen down to our own time.

One of the most fascinating of the assortment of early documents, and one which throws the clearest light on how our ancestors ordained their lives, must surely be the Irish laws, popularly known as the Brehon Laws, because they were administered by the Irish brehons or judges. These laws come down to us from pre-Christian times and were in operation in all parts of Ireland outside the English Pale up to the time of Henry VIII. They continued to be observed in some parts of the country for almost another two hundred years, but by the close of the 17th century the professions of brehon and *ollamh* had become extinct, and the laws fell into disuse. These laws, together with early literature and legends, fill in the picture and give us tantalising glimpses of the early hermit in the fastness of his rocky island, subduing his passions on a meagre diet of dry bread and watercress; of the sons of princes and chieftains in fosterage enjoying their bread and honey; of the baker producing the woman's cake, daintier and smaller than the one served to men; of the crafty Bricriu ordering his servants to prepare the champion's portion (roast boar, fine wine and a hundred honey cakes) in an endeavour to stir up trouble amongst his guests.

In the early literature one particular story not only treats of bread-baking and the dilemma of the housewife caught out at the arrival of the unexpected visitor but also tells of rivalry and jealousy, and of the arrogance of the surly servant aping the manners of his "betters" in the days when a king or overlord could send his soldiers and minions on billet to the humblest home.

The story describes how a servant arrived at a certain house on the borders of Munster and Leinster, demanding his supper, and how the woman of the house gave him the loaf she had baked for her ploughman husband. She then baked a second loaf, and when it was cooked the servant, lounging by the fire, expressed the pious hope that it would taste better than the one he had consumed. This enraged the woman, for she considered herself a light hand with the bread; besides which, the churlish fellow had uttered no word of thanks for his supper. "What is it to you?" she demanded angrily, "You have had your share." "Indeed it is my business," he growled, "for the loaf you gave me was but a snack. The one you have just baked is my chief portion. Know you, woman, I am on billet from the king of Munster." The Leinster woman was not to be trifled with. She had met his like before and she was tired of these foreigners, as she termed the rough Munster menials, descending upon her without warning and arrogantly ordering her around. The kitchen and pantry and dairies were her domain and even her husband, a man of uncertain temper, understood this. "This cake," she said sharply, "is my husband's supper. He likes his food and dislikes your kind. Give your king a message from me. Tell him to keep his hirelings at home. We want no more of this billeting nonsense." She took the cake out of the pot-oven and placed it on the window sill to cool. "Take care you don't touch this baking of mine for it is under the protection of the king of Leinster."

This was too much for the greedy churl, who snatched up the cake and tore off a heel. "O loaf, thou art in danger," he mocked, stuffing bread into his mouth. "Thou shalt go after thy fellow. The protection of the king of Leinster shall not save you."

As was to be expected, the woman complained long and bitterly to her husband and he in a rage and hungry to boot, went to his overlord to demand that something be done—a complaint which was duly passed on to the Leinster court. Accusations and countercharges flew between the two kings, who had always disliked each other. Hard words were followed by blows and the upshot was that three great battles were fought between the Leinster men and the men of Munster, and many young lives were lost. "And all because of a greedy servant," noted the scribe in the *Book of Leinster*, "and a loaf of bread."

The early literature mentions the utensils used in baking bread: the sieve (*criathar*), the trough (*losaid*) used for kneading and the griddle (*lann*), as well as a wooden slice or shovel for turning the bread. Corn was ground into meal, sifted to obtain a finer flour, and the dough kneaded in the trough.

The type of grains used in bread-baking had a social significance. Wheaten bread was rated more highly than oaten or barley bread. If a distinction could be made between the types of bread used it might be said that wheaten bread was better known in the south and east of the country, while oaten bread was used almost exclusively in the north and west, where the land might not be as fertile and the living harder.

Barley bread was associated with hardship and penance in the lives of the early saints. St Finian of Clonard, St Molaise of Devenish, St Maedoc of Ferns, St Ciarán of Saigher and countless more holy men fasted on barley bread and water on week-days and feasted on wheaten bread, salmon and ale on Sundays and feast days.

According to legend the young Colm Cille about whom so many apocryphal stories are told, learned his alphabet happily by having the letters formed on the oaten cake which his nurse gave him to eat, a ploy which many hard-pressed mothers have used since time immemorial.

An early law lays down rules for quantities of food and drink to be consumed in monasteries, possibly at the instigation of an abbot who wished to have a sober community: "While clerics and laymen should receive equal quantities of bread, laymen should get twice as much ale."[1] Even the weight and dimensions of a cake of bread were spelled out. The *bairgin banfuine*—woman's cake—was two fists in breadth and a fist in thickness; the *bairgin ferfuine*— man's cake—was twice the size of a woman's cake. There was even a special cake named the *bairgin indriub* which the mistress of the house kept for guests, before whom a cut loaf should never be placed.

For festive occasions, dough was mixed with honey to make a sweet cake, and indeed to have surfeit of honey for such luxuries as honey cakes was lauded by poets. Sharper flavourings too were often used. An English traveller in Ireland in 1600 noted:

> In cities they have such bread as ours, but of a sharp
> flavour, and some mingled with aniseeds and baked like
> cake, and that only in houses of the better sort.[2]

Bread was considered the best talisman against hunger. In Irish folk belief it was considered unlucky to waste bread or indeed to treat it with other than respect. In parts of the country the scrap of dough kept from one baking to leaven the next batch was known as the "blessed bread". Two crusts of bread were used instead of coins to close the eyes of a dead gypsy or itinerant. A traveller should always carry a crust in his pocket lest he stumble on the "hungry grass" and expire of hunger. In folk tradition the "hungry grass" was said to hold the unmarked grave of a famine victim or to be a spot where a dead body had touched the ground or where a meal had been eaten and no crumbs left behind for the people of the otherworld. Bread had a special significance in burial and death customs. On *Bealtaine*—May Day—the beginning of summer, when magic was rife and the use of spells and incantations widespread, special cakes were baked and offered to the dead or given to beggars in the name of the dead.

Again, on the eve of All Souls' Night, 1 November, which

marked the beginning of winter, it was customary to leave bread and water on the kitchen table at midnight for the return of the dead.

Still another belief that had to do with grave goods was still being observed up to recent times. At a certain funeral which took place in Co Limerick in 1970 a grave was opened in error. Before filling it in again the gravediggers sprinkled a loaf with holy water and placed it in the hole. The reason given was that the rest of those who were buried in that spot had been broken. They were brought back by mistake and must now return to where they had come from and would need food for that journey.[3]

In Irish tradition wakes were an important social occasion at which courtships might commence and marriages were sometimes arranged. Neighbours and friends gathered in the house of the dead to pay their last respects; the corpse was laid out in the parlour or best room, otherwise in the kitchen or a newly painted barn. Funeral meats were baked and it was usual to make a special cake. Whiskey, poteen, beer, porter, port wine and tea were provided, and clay pipes of tobacco and snuff for the men and older women. The night was passed in storytelling and the playing of forfeits and wake games.

John Dunton, in his 17th-century *Letters*, describing a Dublin wake, wrote:

> About midnight most of the company being gathered, great platters of boiled flesh were brought into the barn and an abundance of bread all made in fine white cakes of wheat flour. I do not mean small cakes, like our saffron buns or biscuits but of the size of a large sieve and near three inches thick, portions of which with meat were distributed to everyone and great tubs of drink which was brewed that day followed on hand-barrows, then came tobacco, pipes and sneezing.[4]

When the swaggering Norman lords first arrived in Ireland at the end of the 12th century they brought with them a vastly different style of living from that of their Irish peers. It was customary amongst the barons and wealthy merchants to serve bread of the first quality with the meat or fish course at meals. Servants and other humble folk might make do with coarser bread. To know the colour of one's bread was to know one's place in society. In the halls of their great castles two hundred or more might sit down to dine. Meals were served at long tables to a noisy, colourful company: knights boasting of prowess at hawking or in the hunting field, their ladies clad in gowns of velvet and silk, wearing high-crowned head-dresses or carefully arranged wimples adorning their curls. A bishop in scarlet robes might be seen condescending to a rich merchant and his buxom wife. And overall was the hum of scurrying servants, the occasional sharp order rapped out by the steward and the intermittent colloquy of the hounds lying negligently at the feet of their masters, so that the lute player or harper plucking the strings in the minstrel's gallery could scarcely be heard above the din.

These Norman lords brought with them retainers who knew their ways and cooks who knew their palates. They introduced new and exotic spiced dishes: roasted head of a boar with tusks served on a silver dish, stuffed sucking pig, great pastry pies, containing fowl and game, cooked with minced beef, marrow, egg yolks, spices, dried fruits and wine; as well, sugar sweetmeats, marzipans, baked custards in pastry with dried fruits, mincemeat and trencher bread.

Trenchers, thick slices of bread four days old, made of wholemeal flour often mixed with rye or barley, were served at table on platters of silver or pewter. The diner heaped meats and fish on to these trenchers and the coarse bread soaked up the surplus gravy or fats. At the end of the meal they were collected in baskets and given to the servants or thrown to the dogs. Sometimes they were given to peasants or beggars at the gate. The poor, to whom hunger was nothing new, were glad to eat the bread, however hard. Thence came the saying, "He is a good trencherman."

Meslin or maslin bread, made of wheat and rye, probably another Anglo-Norman innovation, was eaten around Kildare, Wexford, Meath and Dublin—counties either in the shadow of the

Pale or under Anglo-Norman influence. In 1790 a Frenchman on a visit to Cork noted: "In the south of Ireland bread is made with oats, in Wicklow with rye and in Meath with a mixture of rye and wheat."[5]

Right down to the 19th century rye bread was still part of the traditional diet. A popular rhyme setting out the excellent properties of the various breads went:

> Rye bread will do you good;
> Barley bread will do you no harm.
> Wheaten bread will sweeten your blood;
> Oaten bread will strengthen your arm.

Another intruder in the Irish bread scene was the "yalla male"—yellow meal—which was introduced to relieve the famines and near-famines of the 19th century. Mixed with white flour in varying proportions it gave a palatable bread, especially if baked thinly on a griddle and eaten hot with butter.

Some kinds of bread were made with little or no hearth equipment. The most primitive methods were to lay the dough directly on the glowing coals or to wrap a small cake in a large leaf and put it down to bake. Tradition dies hard, and Maura Laverty in her book *Never no More* describes how her grandmother, a superb cook, made ash cakes of yellow meal as late as the 1920s in the kitchen of her house on the edge of the Bog of Allen:

> She scalded the Indian meal with salted boiling water, made it into a dough, rolled it thinly and cut it into little scones. A bed was made on the hearth by raking amongst the ashes on all sides. Each scone was rolled in a cabbage leaf and placed on the bed with hot ashes piled on top and left until cooked. The scorched leaf was then turned back to disclose fragrant little cakes which were delicious with rasher gravy and egg yolk.[6]

The most common method of open baking was to heat the

flagstone by means of a sod of turf, which was then wiped clean and the raw cake laid down to bake. However, the more usual method of baking the oaten cake was on a stand before the fire, usually a three-pronged stick called *maide an bhocaire* or the *crágachán*, which included the three-legged stool upon which the stick and cake were supported. At times this method of baking could give rise to confusion, as when a small Donegal boy, when asked by the local priest "And what had you for supper, my boy?" replied, "Oaten bread, your reverence." "And what had you to the bread?" persisted the questioner (meaning what did you eat with it). To which the puzzled youngster replied, "The leg of a stool and a sod of turf, your reverence."

In 1681, Thomas Dinley gave the diet of the vulgar Irish as potatoes, new milk, whey, curds and a large brown oatcake a foot and a half broad, baked before an open fire. He adds, "They use wheat or rye for great days."[7]

Some of the baking stands were made of iron and handsomely embellished, and some were made of stone, which could be well warmed before the bread was laid on it to ensure an even heat. Bread baked in a wall-oven or in a pot-oven or bastable was usually leavened. The bastable, which was to be found in every Irish rural homestead, takes its name from Barnstaple in Devon, where these iron baking pots were made. During the baking the pot was hung over the fire, or rested on a trivet or on its own legs with coals underneath and piled high on top. It could equally be used to cook a pot roast and it ensured a good even heat. When the bread was taken out of the bastable it was left on its side on the window ledge to cool.

From time immemorial women were the chief bread-makers, though in medieval monasteries bread was baked by monks, in wall-ovens. These ovens were heated by inserting red-hot coals and when the proper temperature was reached the bread was put down to bake. This was a quick and economical way of producing large batches of bread, for the monks were responsible for feeding not only the community but also the patients in the hospices which were attached to monasteries, as well as the beggars and itinerants who called daily to the kitchens.

One of the oldest of all leavens is the sourdough method, and like many great discoveries it probably came about by accident. An old fable describes what happened. Long ago in the "stone age" when a woman made bread by the simple expedient of mixing ground corn and water together and baking the dough on hot stones or in the fire, a young girl had just put down a loaf to bake when her lover invited her to go on a hunting trip. Off she sped, leaving the mixing bowl unwashed. When next she went to mix a cake in the bowl, a lump of sour fermented dough from the last baking was mixed in with the new dough. The result, of course, was delicious spongy bread which gained her the reputation of being the best bread-maker in Ireland, to her immense satisfaction. Even her lover had to admit that she was a better cook than his mother.

Barm beer or liquid yeast obtained from beer-brewing was used from early times. Sowans (fermented juice of oat husks) was another traditional leaven, as was potato juice (potatoes grated and the juice allowed to turn sour). Bread soda, which would act not only as a leavening agent, but create the traditional soda bread, did not come into use until the first half of the 19th century. Cream of tartar and commercial baking powders continue to be used down to the present time.

It is understandable that Irish women were always proud of their potato and boxty (*bacstaí*) cakes; they might argue that the potatoes grown in Ireland were more floury than those grown elsewhere, or that long experience had taught them just how much melted butter or milk to add to the mixture. What is less clear is why Irish country soda bread became synonymous with traditional bread-making in so short a time. It may have had to do with the fresh, thick buttermilk which was always used in the baking, or the flour used, or the light hand of the baker. Certainly no bread ever tasted sweeter or nuttier than that baked in a pot-oven among the ashes of a turf fire.

Of all the puddings made for the various festivals the most delicious was "beesting" pancakes, made with the strippings or beestings of the newly calved cow. In the Clogher Valley of Tyrone they had a saying:

No Shraft without a weddin',
No Hallow Eve without a pudden'.

Spongy griddle cakes with cold bacon were brought out to
workers in the field with pitchers of buttermilk at harvest time,
while turf-cutters got cakes made with curds and cream. Bread
made with goat's milk, called "goaty bread", was also eaten.
Gingerbread was sold at markets and fairs and given to children
as a treat. An old-fashioned and delicious gingerbread was made
with sugar, eggs and treacle, beaten together. In another bowl
butter was melted and mixed with hot water, and this was added
to the egg mixture and again well beaten. Flour, salt, bread soda
and spices were sifted together and folded into the mixture, which
was placed in a baking dish. A spicy, buttery fruit topping was
made by mixing together a little brown sugar, cinnamon, flour,
butter and a handful of raisins. These combined together to
become a crumbly mixture which was spread over the cake before
it was baked.[8]

The bride cake or wedding cake was much less rich than the
iced plum cake of today. Often it was no more than a simple
wheaten cake or one made with honey and fruit, but it was an
important part of the wedding feast because it denoted prosperity
and good fortune. When the bride entered her home after the
marriage ceremony her mother broke the cake over her head for
luck, and then divided the pieces amongst the guests. In the Pale
of Dublin and the Anglo-Norman strongholds of the east, servant-
maids used to bake a rich plum cake decorated with almond paste,
called simnel cake, which they took home on Mothering Sunday,
that is, the Sunday before Lent began. Simnel was originally a
spiced bread, probably introduced here by the Elizabethan settlers
of the 16th century. If the maid was unable to bake her cake, her
sweetheart might get one baked and then present it with the verse:

And I'll to thee a simnel bring
For when thou goes a-mothering;

So when thy mother blesses thee
Half the blessing thou'll give to me.

James Joyce, in the funeral scene in *Ulysses*, describes hawkers selling simnel cakes outside Glasnevin cemetery in Dublin in the early part of the century. Small griddle cakes smeared with treacle, called *gátairí* were also sold on the streets of Dublin and at country fairs and markets. Saffron cakes were eaten on Good Friday and were also given to children suffering from measles (the cure was said to be in the saffron).

The introduction of white bread and tea to the ordinary household of the second half of the 19th century changed the diet pattern of the Irish, and home-baked wheaten bread suffered a decline (a trend which happily has now been reversed). Tea and white bread were always produced for special occasions such as the priest's breakfast the day of the Stations, and white bread soon became known as the priest's bread.

A fine summer evening, music to lift your heart, the dancers gathering at the crossroads and on top of a dash-churn a fine cake, decorated with wild flowers, ringed round with whatever fruit was in season—it is small wonder that the cake dance is remembered in folk tradition as a most joyous occasion and that the custom which was so widespread lingered on down to the present century.

Traditionally the cake dance was held on Easter Sunday, on Whit Sunday, on "pattern" day to celebrate the beginning of summer, on the gathering of the harvest or indeed on almost any fine Sunday evening, when the day's work was done.

The cake could be a griddle, barley or oaten bannock, or best of all a currant loaf or barm brack. If times were good it might be an elaborate affair, decorated with animals or birds raised on the crust. Invariably the cake was prominently displayed on top of a milk churn or dash on which a fine cloth of white linen had first been spread. All the neighbours assembled, the young people took their places, the musicians struck up the opening bar of music and the dance began. The winners might be adjudged the pair who were the lightest on their feet or the couple who could dance longest or the most handsome couple or the pair who had just announced their plans to marry. To them fell the honour of "taking the cake", which they divided out amongst their friends.

The cake dance goes back to medieval times or even earlier and is certainly strong in folk memory. The earliest written account describes a cake dance held in Co Westmeath some time around 1682:

> On the patron day in most parishes, as also on the feasts of Easter and Whitsuntide, the more ordinary sort of people meet near the ale house in the afternoon at some convenient spot of ground and dance for a cake…The cake is provided at the charge of the ale wife and is advanced on a board on top of a pike about ten foot high; this board is round and from it rises a kind of garland, tied with meadow flowers if it be early summer. If later the garland has the addition of apples set in round pegs fastened into it. All dance in a large ring around the bushes they call the garland, and they that hold out the longest win the cake and the apples.[9]

Often an enterprising shopkeeper or inn-keeper might present a rich plum cake in the hope of encouraging business. In the *Dublin Evening Post* of 1 October 1734 the following notice appeared :

> On Thursday next Mary Kelly at the Queen's Head in Glasnevin near this city [Dublin] will have a fine plum cake to be danced for by the young men and maidens of the country who are generously invited by her, no doubting but they will be as pleased with her ale as they are with her cake.[10]

Garlic bread is no newcomer to the Irish culinary scene. From early times many condiments were used with bread. The old Irish law tracts define kitchening as the relish which should accompany each loaf: "four stalks of garlic to each cake, or honey or fish or bacon, with an inch of fat, salted venison or pork, eggs or fish, curds or salted bones."

But whether people ate wheaten bread, oaten bread, meslin bread, or barley bread; bread made with maize or yellow meal, with potatoes, apples or bilberries, or the much-loved barm brack, it was against the laws of hospitality to economise on butter.

Rich, golden home-made butter has always been the favourite accompaniment to bread. When times were good it was on every table, served at every meal and enjoyed on festive occasions. Even when times were bad it was always given to visitors. Bearing all this in mind, the *Annals of Ireland* under the date 1486 describe the demise of one who was surely the meanest man of his day. This is how the scribe wrote the obituary that still has a sting after five hundred years :

> Neidhe O'Mulconry, head of the Inhospitality of Ireland died. He it was who solemnly swore that he would never give bread and butter to his guest.[11]

REFERENCES

1. *Ancient Laws of Ireland*, III.
2. L Falkinder, *Illustrations of Irish History and Topography*, London, 1904, 321.
3. Department of Irish Folklore, MS 1907, 367.
4. In Edward MacLysaght, *Irish Life in the 17th Century*, Dublin, 1939, 359.
5. *Journal of the Cork Historical and Archaeological Society*, LXXI, 1974, 16.
6. Maura Laverty, op. cit., 86.
7. Thomas Dinley, *Observations in a Tour through the Kingdom of Ireland in 1681*, Dublin, 1870, 337.
8. Department of Irish Folklore. MS 2066, 102.
9. *Béaloideas*, XI, 1941, 127.
10. *Journal of the Old Athlone Society*, II, 1972-73, 123.
11. The Four Masters, op. cit.

8

The Land of Youth

Legendary stories tell of a shadowy island far out to the west, which could be glimpsed now and again before it disappeared into the waves. Many intrepid sailors set out in search of its fabled shores but no one ever succeeded in his quest. It was known by various names: Hy Brasil, *Tír Tairngire* or the Land of Promise, *Tír na nÓg* or the Land of Youth, and most evocative of all, *Maigh Meala* or the Plain of Honey. This Otherworld of the Irish was known as a place of music and laughter, of warm streams, golden apples, fine wines and choicest mead, and of golden-haired people, where, in the words of the poet W B Yeats: "nobody grows old and crafty and wise, where nobody gets old and bitter of tongue."[1] A land of milk and honey was how many poets and storytellers liked to describe Ireland down through the "golden ages", no doubt basing their vision on the shadowy paradise of their pagan ancestors. However, there is little doubt that while streams did not flow with wine, or golden apples hang from every bough, there was milk and honey in abundance from earliest times.

Sugar was a rare and costly commodity for many centuries, and indeed almost unknown in Europe until some shrewd Venetian entrepreneurs saw its possibilities and began to open up trade in Europe in the Middle Ages. Down the centuries there had been the occasional brief mention of sugar by soldiers and crusaders. The Persians, reaching the river Indus in 510 BC, called

the sugar cane "the reeds which produce honey without bees."
Alexander the Great knew of it, so too did the Romans; the first
crusaders saw it growing in Syria, and Marco Polo tells how he was
impressed by the sugar mills of China in 1300. However, it took a
Norman baron to introduce sugar into Ireland in the form of a rare
and costly sweetmeat shortly after the coming of Strongbow at the
end of the 12th century. It was to be many more centuries before
sugar would appear on the tables of the common folk. Meanwhile
there was golden, heather-flavoured honey, to be used in cooking
meat and fish, to make delicious honey cakes without which no
kingly banquet was complete, and, above all, to be used in the
making of mead, one of the oldest beverages in the world.

So important was honey in early Ireland that a special section
of the Brehon Laws was devoted to bees and beekeeping. Tributes
to kings and chieftains were paid in honey; in the section on
fosterage in the Laws it was laid down that the food to be given
to sons and daughters of princes and chieftains should include
honey. Less privileged children might make do with porridge and
buttermilk, but the sprigs of the mighty were to get porridge served
with as much honey as they could eat. Provision was also made
for every contingency that might arise in beekeeping. The owner
of a hive of bees was obliged to distribute a supply of honey to his
neighbours every three years because the bees would have gathered
nectar on their land. Provision too was made for every possible sort
of swarming, whether in a tree, in a wood, a lake or other wild place,
within an enclosure, a green or in a herb garden. There was even
a penalty laid down for the owner of a hive if one of his bees stung
an unwary passer-by. The victim was entitled to a full meal of honey
as recompense.

The abundance of honey in early Ireland can be measured from
the size of the vessels used either to collect the honeycombs or to
pay tribute to an overlord, or for kitchen use. A barrel so large and
heavy that it could only be lifted as far as the knees by a man of
strength (presumably when it was full of honey) was used, or a
smaller vessel that could be raised on the shoulder and head. Not
alone was honey used in cooking but at table each person had a

dish of honey into which he dipped his portion of meat, fowl or fish.

Royal Tara, the seat of kings and princes, where heroes were feted, contained, according to legend, the mead banqueting hall, where great feasts were held and each man drank to capacity of the golden heather-flavoured nectar of the gods. Mead flavoured with hazelnuts was a drink to remember. One of the three great sorrows of Irish storytelling is *The Fate of the Children of Lir*, in which Fionnuala and her three brothers are turned into swans by their jealous stepmother. Fionnuala looks back sadly on their former life when, at the court of their royal father, they drank hazel mead. And in the 10th-century story of King Guaire the hospitable, we read that one of the joys of the hermit's life was a cup of hazel mead.

Honey and mead played their part in the lives of the early saints. That there were wild bees in Ireland seems proven by one of the many legends told of the childhood of St Ciarán of Clonmacnoise. One day Ciarán's mother said to him, "All the little lads of the hamlet bring honey out of the honeycombs to their households, except you." On hearing this Ciarán went to a certain well and filled his vessel with water, which he blessed so that it turned into honey. He brought this home to his mother, who was no doubt vastly impressed, convinced that her son was cleverer and kinder than any of his companions, as so many mothers before and since have thought.

Some of the early legends of the saints, as well as authorities such as the scribe Solinus in the 2nd century AD (nicknamed "Pliny's ape" because of the use he made of the writings of Pliny the Elder), affirmed that Ireland originally had no bees. But there seems little doubt that bees, both wild and domesticated, were to be found in Ireland at a very early time. Whether or not Ireland possessed native bees, tradition would have us believe that a 6th-century saint, Madomnoc, patron of Tibberaghny and Fiddown, Co Kilkenny, first brought bees to Ireland from Wales. The story of the coming of the little brown bees is full of charm. According to the legend the youthful Madomnoc set out for Wales to study at the feet of the great St David. He remained many years in the monastery, where his special care was the beehives which formed part of the great abbey's wealth. Now when at length the time came for Madomnoc to return home his little friends refused to be parted from him. Three times they followed him to the ship waiting to set sail for Ireland and three times he bore them back to their hives. In the end St David, ever generous, presented the swarm of bees to his friend and disciple. He blessed the bees with the words: "May the land to which you are brought abound with your progeny and may their species and generation never fail, but our own city shall be forever deprived of you, nor shall your seed any longer increase in it." The prophecy was fulfilled, for the British bees prospered and multiplied in their new home, their honey was ever sweet and the green forests of Ireland were perfumed by that sweetness, but no bees were afterwards found in the monastery of Menevia where David ruled. It was said that after Madomnoc arrived in Ireland the bees that accompanied him were left at Fingal, near Balbriggan, and the name of the foundation was the Church of the Beekeepers. Lovers of bees and honey might wish to know that the feast-day of Madomnoc falls on 13 February.

If St Madomnoc is credited with the introduction of bees to Ireland, St Gobnait of Ballyvourney, Co Cork, is regarded as the patron saint of beekeepers. Her feast, like Madomnoc's, occurs in the month of February, and like him, she is reputed to have lived some time in the 6th century. The legend of her dealing with bees is told in many parts of Munster and many variants of the story are contained in the manuscript material of the Department of Irish Folklore. The story goes that an invading chief and his army descended on the country around Ballyvourney with plunder in mind. They would despoil the land and rob the cattle. But they reckoned without Gobnait, for, like the great St Brigid, she was a redoubtable woman. She met the would-be despoilers and robbers holding in her hand a beehive. She prayed for guidance and then let loose the bees. According to some accounts the bees turned into soldiers and routed the enemy; others affirm that the bees stung the marauding chieftain and his followers so sharply that the cowardly fellows fled for their lives. Their work done, the bees dutifully returned to the hive and the making of honey.[2]

Perhaps the most appealing of all the legends connected with bees is taken from a medieval manuscript written by a Franciscan of the Irish Province in the 13th century. He is reputed to have got it from Giraldus Cambrensis.

The legend is entitled "The Priest and the Bee" and tells of how a certain priest set out to tend a dying man, taking with him the Sacred Host. A swarm of bees came his way and, forgetting his errand, he laid aside the Host, gathered up the bees and returned home. However, the little creatures left him, went back to where the Host lay on a greensward, and bore it away. In a sheltered spot they made a chapel of fair wax and a chalice of wax and a pair of waxen priests and made the Host reverence. And the legend relates how the priest was astonished and delighted and brought many people to see the marvellous sight.[3]

A belief once held in many parts of the country was that if a death occurred in a household it was important to go down to the hive and tell the bees; if not they would either swarm elsewhere or die in the hives. Another belief was that you should never buy bees, but let them come to you. It was said that if you liked bees they would come, if not they would keep away.[4]

REFERENCES

1. WB Yeats, *The Land of Heart's Desire, Collected Plays*, London, 1934.
2. Department of Irish Folklore, MS 1139, 270; MS 947, 100; MS 283, 9; MS 302, 92; MS 1137, 226.
3. *British Society of Franciscan Studies*. I, Aberdeen, 1908, and JS Brewer (ed.), *Rerum Britannicarum* II, London, 1862.
4. Department Of Irish Folklore, MS 970 and MS 1639, 329.

9

Sixty Cows with Red Horns

In ancient and medieval Ireland milk and milk products, generally referred to as *bán-bhia* or white-meat, played a central role in the diet of the Irish people. These included every possible gradation of milk: fresh milk, sour milk, thick or ropy milk, buttermilk, cream, butter, curds and cheese. Even after the general adoption of the potato from the 17th century onwards, milk continued to be used in considerable quantities. Probably no other Irish food was the subject of so many customs, traditions and superstitions. One reason was that from prehistoric times down to our own century a healthy stock and an abundance of milk could make all the difference between prosperity and poverty. If cattle failed or the milk yield was poor the more unsophisticated tended to blame forces outside their control, such as magic, witchcraft or the machinations of the fairies or people of the Otherworld, as they were known

Milk has always been a much-loved food, and is mentioned time and again in legendary tales, in the early lives of saints, and by observers and commentators on the Irish scene. In the early 12th-century wonder tale, the hungry and weary Armagh student Mac Conglinne, doodling an idle hour away drawing on the margin of his parchment a green cat, a purple cow, a goat with four horns, and a flying fish, suddenly decides that life is passing him by. Throwing caution to the wind, he gathers up his cloak and leather satchel and with mounting excitement points his shoes of sevenfold dun leather due south. He will make for the court of the Munster king, where he hopes to find sport and adventure, as well as plenty to eat. For, as the story explains, "greedy and hungry for white-meats was the scholar." Over four hundred years later, the traveller and writer John Stevens noted:

> The Irish are the greatest lovers of milk I have ever met, which they eat and drink in about twenty different ways, and what is strangest they love it best when it is sourest.[1]

Luke Gernon, another observer of the scene, wrote in the same century:

> I will not lead you into the baser cabins where you shall have no drink but bonnyclabber [*bainne clabair*], milk that is soured to the condition of buttermilk.[2]

The milk of the deer, of goats and of sheep is frequently mentioned in the early literature. In pre-Christian times, when the legendary Nia Ségamain held sway, hinds and cattle were milked in the same manner each day.[3] Nia Ségamain may never have existed. It was the name given to a Gaulish god by the Celts, and appears on ogham stones, but the account does seem to suggest that the custom of milking the deer was known from ancient times. Again, in the *Tripartite Life*[4] we read how St Patrick met three brothers and a sister in the ancient Abbey of Boyle, Co Roscommon, and we are told that it was the sister who milked the hinds.

The use of sheep's milk has a long history in Ireland. In the *Lismore Lives*[5] it is related that when St Brigid went to visit Cill Laisre, she found the monks using sheep's milk. Mac Conglinne mentions porridge made of sheep's milk. Sheep's milk was used by those who could not afford to keep a cow in the 18th and 19th centuries, and even later. At the turn of this century sheep's milk was used in Tralee, Co Kerry.

> Before the land improved this was sheep's country and the
> local fair was practically a sheep fair. Sheep's milk was used
> at one time. They used a mixture of sheep's milk and butter
> for supper at their stopping places en route [to the town
> or fair to sell butter].[6]

Another account from Cremore, Co Monaghan, shows that milk
puddings made of sheep's milk were considered something of a
luxury, rather like Mac Conglinne's fair white porridge.

> Long ago when the farmer finished gathering in his
> harvest in the Autumn he had a party called a Harvest
> Home in his barn. To this all the neighbours and those
> who took part in the saving of the crops were invited.
> Dancing and fun was indulged in and among the special
> items of food for the occasion was a whole-cooked rice
> made with sheep's milk in an oven pot [dutch oven] with
> red turf embers on top of the lid and underneath the pot.
> Yolks of eggs were whipped and poured over the top and
> this gave a tasty top to the rice pudding. Sheep's milk was
> deemed most nourishing, though it had something of a
> strong flavour.[7]

Goat's milk was always said to be most nutritious of all, good
for children and invalids, especially those suffering from
tuberculosis. (This may be because the goat, unlike the cow, is
immune to the disease; goats also crop herbs in fields and ditches.)
Many farmers kept a goat to run with the cows, and children were
taught to milk the goat. Well into the middle of this century goat's
milk was sold on the outskirts of Dublin, and people travelled
miles to a particular dairy in Rathfarnham to obtain a supply. In
Ardee, Co Louth, goat's milk was said to cure anaemic complaints.

> One half of lamb's liver, two red beets, boiled slowly in
> goat's milk; given to weaklings to drink. Spices or herbs
> added.[8]

The low-fat milk or skim milk popular today with the health-conscious is no innovation. Our ancestors brought sound common sense to everything they did, including what they ate and drank. Full-cream milk was rarely if ever drunk, except by the young, the elderly or the ill. Adults invariably drank skim milk or buttermilk. However, the young need fresh sweet milk for growing bones, and strong teeth, as well as for the energy and sense of well-being it gives, and it is interesting to note that from time immemorial children up to the age of nine or ten years were fed *leamhnacht* or fresh milk. As they got older they were gradually introduced to mixed milk: two thirds sweet milk and one third sour milk. This last was not sour milk as we know it today but the milk left over in the timber churn when the *bainne géar*—sour whole milk—had been churned and the butter removed. As a rule the separating was done twice a day, except in winter and early spring. The addition of the churned milk made a very pleasant drink, wholesome and easy to digest with a slight flavour of tartness: "something to go down through your tongue," as the saying goes.

Thick or ropy milk was obtained when the cream was skimmed off the pans of fresh milk, then left to set for two or three days in the dairy. The taste for thick or ropy milk goes back to early times. Our old friend Mac Conglinne dreams of a delectable drink of

> very thick milk, of milk not too thick, of yellow bubbling milk, the swallowing of which needs chewing so that the first draught says to the last, I vow thou mangy cur before our Creator if thou comest down I'll go up for there is no room for the doghood pair of us in this treasure house.[9]

Fresh buttermilk, the milk left in the churn when the butter was made, was the most refreshing drink in the world. A visitor to the house was invariably offered a mug of buttermilk, straight from the churn. During haymaking, turf-cutting and general harvesting, buttermilk was considered the best drink for slaking thirst, and gave new energy to continue the work. It was customary while turf-cutting to immerse a can of buttermilk in the bog to keep it cool and fresh. Buttermilk was considered a certain cure for a hangover and was much in demand after weddings, wakes and festivals where some were in the habit of imbibing not wisely if too well.

Irish girls washed their faces in buttermilk to improve their complexions, while their mothers and grandmothers put it to a more prosaic use in the baking of bread. If no buttermilk was available a can or saucepan of freshly skimmed milk was put beside the fire to sour before it was used for baking. Buttermilk made an epicurean feast of such simple meals as colcannon, champ, and boiled potatoes served with fish or cabbage and bacon. Fresh milk, heated, sweetened and well flavoured with either ginger, pepper, nutmeg, or a good dollop of Irish whiskey was a favourite nightcap with the elderly or the ailing, and considered an infallible cure for insomnia, while hot milk and honey had a soothing effect on the nerves, and was much in demand in the days before tranquillisers. Another old-fashioned and well-attested cure was garlic-flavoured milk (a clove of garlic was set in a saucepan of milk which was brought almost to boiling point, when the garlic was removed). A tried and tested cure for a bad wetting was to soak one's feet in hot water, then take a nightcap of hot milk, honey and Irish whiskey.

One of the plagues of medieval Ireland was leprosy, which milk, if it did not cure, certainly helped. A story in the *Early Lives* relates how two lepers came to St Brigid for aid. She had only one cow, which she gave them as a joint gift. One leper praised her bounty, the second, a mean and covetous person, took off with the cow, which he drove over the dry section of the Liffey bed. When he was half-way across, the waters of the river rose up and drowned both man and animal. The story concludes that Brigid got another cow which she gave to the grateful leper and that he went his way blessing her charity.

As a young girl Brigid was fostered by the Chief Druid. His wife, jealous of the fosterling's beauty and goodness, came to the dairy one day and ordered the full of a hamper of butter, knowing that Brigid had given away most of the milk to beggars. "See that you do as I say or it will be the worse for your slave mother," the woman mocked. In desperation Brigid prayed:

> Mary's son, please help my need.
> Send butter enough for my mistress's greed.

The legend tells us that God heard the prayers of Brigid and that from the little milk she had she churned enough butter to feed all the people of Leinster.

Curds, a popular food, made by boiling sour and sweet milk together, were said to be a cure for colds, stomach upsets and other minor ailments. In the 17th century the writer and traveller Dunton described the hospitality of the peasants in Iar-Chonnacht.

> The next morning a great pot full of new milk was set over the fire to heat which was then poured into a pail of buttermilk which made a mighty dish of tough curds. In the middle the woman of the house placed a pound weight of butter.[10]

This was considered a delicacy and very nourishing.

Curds made from the milk of a cow that had just calved were known as beestings. One of the blessings of the good King Cormac Mac Airt's reign was that cows had udders full of beestings. And in the year 942 when Muircheartach of the Leather Cloak made his famous circuit of Ireland with his warriors,

> they were restored to health and well being when they returned to Tara with three score vats of curds which banished the hungry look of the army.[11]

Curds, like butter and cattle, were used in early Christian Ireland as tribute or rent. In the *Tripartite Life*[12] we read that on a certain day the overlord sent a demand for rent in the form of curds and butter to St Patrick's foster mother, though it was winter and the cows were dry. Patrick, knowing she was upset because of this impossible demand, prayed to God for guidance. Outside the skies were overcast and snow fell heavily, silently mantling the Slemish mountains so that not a creature was to be seen. Patrick went out and made a basket of snow, which turned into one of rushes, then he moulded snow into shapes, balls and slabs and these turned into curds and butter. The basket of white-meats was taken to the overlord, who was pleased to accept them for such viands were rare in winter. He set the basket of curds and butter on the supper table but as he did so the lot turned back into snow. The servants, frightened of Patrick's power, told their master what had happened, and the overlord, not wishing to incur the wrath of so powerful a man, remitted the rent and did not trouble that household again.

Meadhg was the generic name for whey, the pale green liquid produced with the curds and which could be either sweet or sour. It was early known as *treabhantar*, or troander. Whey was in constant use in medieval monasteries and is mentioned in the list of foods allowed the Culdee monks. The scholar Mac Conglinne, in his *Vision of a Land of Plenty*,[13] grumbled at the miserly reception given him in the Cork monastery where the monks gave him whey water to drink and nothing else.

Whey was said to have excellent curative properties, and the two-milk whey, made with sweet milk and sour milk, or sweet milk and buttermilk, was widely used as a folk cure all over the country up to this century. The most common recipe was to bring three-quarters of a pint of new or fresh milk to boiling point, then to add about one-eighth of a pint of buttermilk and stir the lot continuously until the curds clotted. The whey obtained had a very light acid taste and could be kept for a couple of days without turning sour. In Co Westmeath it was considered an excellent cure for a cold with sugar and whiskey added, while in Beara, Co Cork, the two-milk whey was given as a cure for kidney ailments. In Carbery in the same county, it was said to cure vomiting and other stomach upsets. In Killenaule, Co Tipperary, whey was made by boiling fresh milk and throwing in a dash of sour milk, and was said to be a good drink for anyone suffering from a fever.[14] It is interesting to remember that Mac Conglinne enticed the demon of gluttony out of the stomach of the diabetic king with curds (and possibly whey).

It is but a small step from curds to cheese. Throughout the whole of the long period from pre-Christian Ireland down to the end of the 18th century cheese was a staple food. According to Dr Lucas in his study of Irish food before the Famine,[15] *cáis*, the Modern Irish word for cheese goes back to ancient times. It is not clear if it was the generic name for cheese or for a particular type.

Most farmhouses had a dairy with rows of shelves of gleaming pans and strainers, where the dairymaid or woman of the house made cheese. Traditional cheeses included *tanach*, a hard-pressed skim-milk cheese; *táth*, a soft cheese made from heated sour milk curds, rather like a cooked Continental cheese; *gruth*, a curdy cheese made from buttermilk or skim milk; *mulchán*, made of buttermilk beaten to form a soft cheese which was then pressed and moulded; and *milseán*, made from sweet milk curds eaten at the end of a banquet or harvest festival. Cream cheese was popular, made with thick rich cream, a pinch of salt and a little dry mustard, all of which were placed in a jelly bag or straining cloth, usually hung between two chairs with a basin underneath to catch the drops. When the cream solidified, which took about twenty-four hours in the cool of the dairy, the cheese was turned into a mould and pressed under a butter-weight until firm.

Various types of cheese are mentioned in the early literature. Queen Méabh of Connacht in her old age was struck on the forehead by a piece of *tanach* or hard cheese, let fly by her nephew Furbaide: a sad ending to the most famous warrior queen in Irish sagas and the instigator of the greatest cattle raid of all, the *Táin Bó Cuailgne*—Cattle Raid of Cooley. Cheese was also used in an attempt on the life of St Patrick according to the *Tripartite Life*.[16] Hui Lilaig, the druid, jealous of Patrick's missionary success and his own waning influence, put poison in a curd cheese and then set out to meet his rival. Patrick, wary of druids when they came bearing gifts, blessed the cheese, which immediately turned into stones. Then, to ensure that Hui Lilaig had got the message, he changed the hard stones back into curds, and once more back into stones; after which the druid retreated in disorder.

Binid was the rennet commonly used in the making of cheese, and was extracted from the stomach of a calf. Rennet was used as far back as the 9th century. The Culdee monks were forbidden to eat cheese because the rennet was extracted from the flesh of an animal. Milk could also be curded by the use of lady's bedstraw, known in Irish as *rú Mhuire* or *baladh chnise*, which was also used as a traditional crimson dyestuff. It gets its name from the charming folk belief that it was one of the herbs in Christ's manger in Bethlehem.

Most cheese was made from cow's milk, though goat's cheese was eaten and considered very nourishing.

Cheese made from sheep's milk has a long history. It is mentioned in the early literature and was still being used on a considerable scale in Kilkenny up to the end of the 19th century. However, like much else that was excellent in traditional food skills, the art of cheese-making declined at the end of the 18th century, and a food for which we were once justly famous was seldom eaten.

While in recent years Irish cheese has greatly increased in quality and consumption, we still have a distance to go to equal the time when we counted among the great cheese-makers of the world and when this most nutritious of foods was to be found on every Irish table.

Before the advent of the creamery every farmhouse had its own churn and all the other dairying implements that went with butter-making: well-scoured crockery pans or wooden bowls in which milk was left to set (anything from a couple of days to a week, depending on room temperature and weather), wooden skimmer, ladles, butter scoops, spades, prints or stamps for decorating the butter with the design of a flower, and pats for rolling pieces of butter into convenient sizes for the table. The most commonly used churn was the dash, made of oak or larch, with a churn staff to agitate the milk. In later times the barrel churn, which rotated on its axis by means of a crank handle, became popular; the tumble or turn-over churn was used in larger farmhouses.

In Letterkenny, Co Donegal, the traditional way of making butter was as follows: skim milk was poured into the churn along with the risen cream, the staff was put in, on went the lid and the work commenced. Very warm work it was too. The staff was worked up and down for an hour and if after that time the butter was plentiful on the top of the milk the job was done. The butter was lifted out of the churn and all traces of milk were washed away. The butter was then salted and weighed. When the butter was shaped and stamped with the design it was taken to the shop for sale once weekly.[17]

In Blacklion, Co Cavan, the butter was lifted off the milk in the churn with the hands, which had been well washed in spring water.

> They had a wee rake, a wee comb, and they'd comb the butter until there wasn't a hair left on it. They'd spill water from a spring well, real cold water and it would stay firm with the coldness. They'd make it into big squares and clap it, and they had a wee article made of wood and they'd put prints on it. If the butter was scalded too much and was very pale and not marketable, it would be coloured. They put grated carrots into a saucepan on the fire, boiled them, strained the juice and spilled a drop or two of carrot juice over the butter and raked it. It was the loveliest you ever tasted. After the churning was finished, the buttermilk was given to friends and neighbours or to farm workers to take home. The woman of the house would drop a portion of butter into the buttermilk can as an extra perk. The butter floated on top of the can and was easily retrieved.[18]

> When milk was breaking on the churn, when it was neither sweet nor sour, when the butter was about to come on it, the old people swore it was a cure for all ills.[19]

The "good people," the "gentlemen of the hills," "the people of the sí, as Irish fairies were variously known, played a very important part in the everyday life of the community in rural Ireland, down to the present day. It is interesting to note that in folk tradition people did not often differentiate between these supernatural creatures and the dead. The late Michael Corduff, national teacher and one of the finest folklorists in the west of Ireland, recorded a fine body of tradition from his native Rossport, Co Mayo, in the 1940s and '50s, and had this to say of Irish fairies.

> The malign influences of the gentlemen of the hills covered much of the people's activities—it was the constant desire of people to propitiate the fairies. This they did in many ways, such as leaving unsalted food for them at night, spilling milk on the ground, casting a morsel of food on the ground when a person sneezed, spilling out the first glass of poteen coming from the still etc. Cattle were particularly susceptible to attacks from the fairies and "good people" and many and varied were the means adopted for protection against them. Stories are told all over Ireland of how cattle and even human beings were taken away by them.[20]

Many superstitions were associated with butter and butter-making. Everything about the churn had to be right. Two different types of wood had to be used in making the crossbeams. These were considered necessary because luck played such an important part in churning. Now and again the butter might mysteriously refuse to "break", a disaster which could be put down to the fact that a witch or neighbour with the "evil eye" had "overlooked" the cow and by infamous means had stolen the butter. To counteract such spells a twig of the rowan tree or quicken tree, known as the fairy-tree was tied to the churn dash, or a piece of salt was dropped into the milk, or a red ribbon or red rag was tied to the cow's tail after calving. A visitor to the house was expected to take a hand with the churning to ensure good luck. A bachelor who was courting a daughter of the house should never lift the butter off the churn: to do so would render him impotent. "Is it your daughter marry the man who took the butter off the churn?" (i.e. made the butter) was a bitter remark. Hags, witches and people of the Otherworld all feared salt and iron and these could be used as safeguards against spells. In Tyrone, the coulter of the plough was put in the fire and a hair rope tied from it to the churn to prevent ill-luck, while in Rossport, Co Mayo, a red-hot iron was placed under the churn for the same reason.[21] A decidedly gruesome way to steal butter and one remembered in living memory was to stir the milk in the churn with the hand of a dead man, preferably one who had died on the gallows, meanwhile naming the person from whom the milk was to be taken.

> They used have a dead hand to take the butter not over a
> hundred miles, just above the Blackwater.[22]

In Co Mayo they put the dead hand of an infant under the churn for the same purpose.

In Kill, Co Galway, a woman and her two daughters lived in a miserable house on an acre of stony ground, and yet they always had plenty of butter, a state of affairs which gave rise to a certain amount of uneasy speculation amongst the neighbours. The mystery was solved when a neighbouring farmer called in to light his pipe just as they were finishing the churning. The woman of the house put her hand down into the churn, took up a huge lump of butter and mentioned Kill (the townland from which she was stealing the butter). She took a second and bigger lump and mentioned another townland. Then she took the biggest lump of all and the man said to himself, "That's the butter of the parish at large." And as he well knew, all the stock she had was two poor wee cows.[23]

To spill milk, whether by accident or design, had a special significance. If milk was kicked over by a cow, the old people would say, "There is maybe a dry hearth waiting for that," meaning that the milk was needed by the fairy folk. In the manuscript material there are many variants of the story of the crying child. A woman is troubled by the wailing of an unseen infant. She confides in an old travelling woman who advises, "When you fill your first pail at milking time this evening, take it out in the bawn and upturn it with your foot." The woman does as she is bid, and the cry of the fairy child is heard no more. Another version from Lough Derravaragh, Co Westmeath, tells of a farmer's wife who heard a child crying, but refused to spill milk. Somewhere nearby a voice said soothingly, "Hush, child, you will have your milk." The farmer's wife drove her cow through the gap in the hedge, and as she did so the animal slipped and broke a leg. It was the fairy's revenge. It was a hard-earned lesson, but the farmer's wife made sure for the future to heed any unseen cry for help, and to spill milk if it was needed.

It was widely held that to spill milk purposely on a neighbour would bring the person named bad luck. Much the same kind of spell was invoked if a sheaf of wheat or oats, a hatching of eggs or a bit of lamb or a hen was buried in another's land. Ruin and disaster would follow, according to an informant in Layde, Co Antrim.[24] However, very often the perpetrator of the nefarious deed had to pay a price. A chilling account of such an occurrence from Ardee, Co Louth, goes:

> My father spilled the milk to try and stop a certain person
> from using the pass in case it would become legal and they
> could claim a right of way. The curse follows us and our
> name and will be gone out of the townland in a few years.
> Seven sons and not one with a male heir.[25]

The narrator finishes up with a quotation from "Wildgoose Lodge", William Carleton's tragic story of the Whiteboys: "Not alone did they cut the looms but they also spilled the milk, and the world knows the rest."[26]

An enchanting legend from the *Lives* tells how St Ciarán of Clonmacnoise was appointed caretaker of the king's gold and herds of cattle when that high and mighty person was called away to settle a dispute at the other end of the country. Now Ciarán, like most Irish saints, could never refuse a request for help, and in the king's absence the crops failed and there was great hardship amongst the common folk. They came begging Ciarán to help, and he distributed all the king's goods in the name of charity. But the day of reckoning was not far off, and when the king eventually returned and heard what had happened his fury made even the queen quake, and that was something no man had ever before witnessed. The king began by promising to have Ciarán flayed alive, and then by sentencing him to a diet of dry bread and bracken water, and finally by threatening to have him banished for life if proper recompense was not made. "Bring me," he thundered, "three score white cows with red horns, or all I have sworn will come to pass." It was an impossible demand, but Ciarán had friends in very high places indeed. He sought out St Ciarán of Saigher and St Brendan, and the three of them together went down on their knees to pray for a miracle, which duly happened with the prompt arrival in the bawn of sixty white cows with proud red horns. Their like had never before been seen in the land. Ciarán drove the herd back to the king, who accepted them rather ungraciously, for he was a difficult man and hard to please. However, he did not long enjoy his wonderful cattle; day by day they faded away until none was left. It was said they were fairy cows and had gone back to their rightful owners in the raths and the hollow hills, an explanation that gave the king pause. Even he had no wish to become entangled with the people of the Otherworld. And as for Ciarán, he continued all his days doing good.

REFERENCES

1. Rev RH Murray (ed.), *The Journal of John Stevens*, 139-142.
2. Luke Gernon, *A Discourse on Ireland*, 1620, 359-360.
3. Stokes and Windisch (eds.), *Cóir Anman Irische Texte*, III, 1897, 285-440.
4. Whitley Stokes (ed. and trans.), *Tripartite Life of St Patrick*, London, 1887.
5. Whitley Stokes, (ed. and.trans.), "Lives of the Saints" from *The Book of Lismore*. Oxford, 1980.
6. Department of Irish Folklore. Questionnaire on Milk and Milk Products, contained in Vols. 1452, 1453, 1565, 1669.

7. Ib., MS 1453, 152.
8. Ib., Questionnaire on Milk.
9. Meyers, op. cit.
10. Dunton, op .cit.
11. *Tracts Relating to Ireland*, 1841.
12. Stokes, op. cit.
13. Meyers, op. cit.
14. Department of Irish Folklore, Questionnaire:Milk.
15. Lucas, op. cit.
16. Stokes, op. cit.
17. Department of Irish Folklore, MS 2046, 77.
18. Ib., MS 1086, 177.
19. Ib., MS 1362, 205.
20. Ib., MS 1072, 40-41.
21. Ib., MS 1806, 187.
22. Ib., MS 1640, 116-117.
23. Ib.
24. Ib., MS 1359, 122.
25. Ib., Questionnaire on Milk.
26. William Carleton, "Wildgoose Lodge" in *Traits and Stories of the Irish Peasantry*, Dublin, 1830-33.

10

Life on the Mountains

Now and again to this very day a turf-cutter or farmer or worker on the land will unearth the remains of a casket of bog butter, thereby uncovering a custom that is not only Irish but international, not only of great antiquity but still surviving in parts of Europe. This custom is known as booleying, or transhumance, that is driving stock to mountain pastures during the summer months. Finds of bog butter frequently occur in districts where booley huts once stood. Bogs, which are cool and antiseptic, were favourite storage places for food, long before fridges or freezing cabinets were invented. Food might thus be stored in times of war or upheaval, but the practice of burying surplus butter, often in a container of sycamore wood, salted, flavoured with garlic or herbs (and sometimes without any additives), was common. It could later be taken up and used in the lean months of winter.

The earliest find of bog butter was at Cullard, Co Roscommon, and dates back to the 6th century AD, but possibly the practice was even earlier. Butter may have been thrown into bog holes or into lakes which preceded the bogs as a form of ritual offering or thanksgiving for favours received in early times.

Dr E Estyn Evans, who has made a study of this subject, says:

> The practice of depositing butter in bogs continued at least
> as late as the 18th century. It seems to me that the custom

may have lingered in remote places down to the Great
Famine. If it was associated, as I am inclined to think it was,
with the booleying tradition, it is not likely to have survived
the break-up of that immemorial way of life.[1]

There were sound reasons why people drove their cattle to
summer pastures: fresh grazing was provided for the cattle, and
fields of clover and good grass abounded on the heights, in addition
to which the home fields where the cattle had wintered could be
used for tillage or meadowing.

Booleying was evidently quite common in the 17th century, for
several writers of the period comment on the practice. Fynes
Moryson tells of the makeshift houses occupied by men herding
and guarding cows on pasture distant from their permanent
settlements,[2] while John Dunton, visiting the O'Flahertie of Iar-
Chonnacht, described him as

the most considerable man in the territory, living with his
relations not in a proper dwelling or mansion house, but
in a booley or summer habitation newly erected on hill
pasture.[3]

Perhaps the most descriptive and attractive account we have of
booleying in living memory comes from a Donegal man, Niall Ó
Dubhthaigh, recorded by the folklorist Seán Ó hEochaidh.[4] Ó
Dubhthaigh describes how his mother as a young girl of thirteen
years first went to pasture the stock with her companions in the
middle of the 19th century. The people had the rights of pasturing
on a mountain some distance away, and it was the custom for the
men and boys to climb the heights of Na Trí Phíopaí on St Patrick's
Day to cut turf and build the small shielings.

On May morning the whole village set out together to accompany
the local girls to the booley where they would spend the summer
months tending the cattle. Provisions had to be brought along,
everything the girls would need from needle and thread to soap
and hairbrush. The moorland tracks were too rough for carts, so

donkeys, panniers slung across their backs, as well as pack horses, were used as transport; what the beasts could not carry the men did. They brought with them milking-cans, tubs and butter-churns, bed linen and stools, pots and pans, crockery, knives and spoons, wool for spinning, and iron rations of flour, potatoes, oatmeal, and salt fish. On the journey the cattle were herded along the mountain track by excited young boys and barking dogs, while each girl carried her own spinning-wheel, combs, and knitting-needle. On November Day, when the potatoes were gathered and the harvest was in, they would leave the mountains and return to their homes. The next week would be spent in visiting the various houses of their companions at the booleying; most nights there would be a "ball" or party in one of the cottages or farmhouses. Perhaps there was a wedding to celebrate, but more often an "American wake", for, sadly, most of the young men were forced in the end to emigrate.

Life on the heights was simple but pleasant. Each little shieling contained a window, a fireplace with a turf-basket, three-legged wooden stools, heather hassocks, and a carpet of green rushes on the floor. The girls slept on beds of rushes, heather, bracken and black mountain sedge, covered with woven linen sheets, woollen blankets and quilts. Black sedges were said to make such a comfortable mattress that a legend grew up around them.

When the Blessed Woman and St Joseph were walking the roads and without a place to lay their heads they were forced to spend the night in a stable, and it was there between the ox and the ass that the Child Jesus was born. The bed of the Holy Family was made of black sedges from the mountains and it was said that ever since anyone sleeping on such a bed never suffered sleeplessness, pain or anxiety but arose the following morning fresh and rested.

The months on the mountains were remembered as idyllic. The girls rose with the dawn and spent their days tending the stock, milking the cows, making butter and cheese, spinning wool and knitting. Food was simple but wholesome. To drink they had an abundance of sweet milk and buttermilk, and to eat oat cakes hot from the griddle with freshly churned butter, as well as curds, oatmeal porridge, potatoes, meat and eggs brought from home, fish

from mountain streams and lakes, and occasionally rabbits, hares
or game snared or brought down by the young men from the
townland, who visited them on Sundays or holiday evenings. Life
on the heights could sometimes be adventurous. A tale is told in
several places of the killing of "the last wolf in Ireland in a summer
pasture."[5]

Butter was made by the girls in common, and in his account of
booleying on a Donegal mountain, Niall Ó Dubhthaigh tells us that
when the butter was sold at the Letterkenny market, whatever the
yield, each girl was paid according to the number of cows her family
owned. None of the butter went astray; it was packed into tubs and
safely stored in little underground houses lined with flagstones,
which the men built and which were as cold as ice-houses. Neither
sun, wind nor rain could penetrate the walls and all summer the
butter remained as firm and hard as an icicle.

In the evenings when the day's work was done, the girls
gathered to spin and tell stories, or sing and dance with the young
men who joined them at weekends or on the great festival of The
Assumption, 15 August. Years later the girls, now grown old,
remembered with delight and nostalgia those sunlit days at the
booleying. But many of the young men who built the shielings and
danced and sported with them left their homes soon after for the
emigrant ship that would take them across the wide Atlantic Ocean
to the New World, some to work in the big cities, some to seek their
fortunes in the land to the west which was opening up and still
more to fight and fall on the battlefield of Gettysburg in the
American Civil War.

Niall Ó Dubhthaigh tells of a poignant link with a young girl
singing on a summer's evening in a shieling high on a Donegal
mountain and a young man in the uniform of a Yankee soldier
falling in battle on the red clay in the deep south:

> It's many the sweet Irish song my mother had and she told
> us that it was in the long ago in the shielings that she heard
> those same songs from this boy or that, fine young men
> who went to America. Some were killed in the great war
> [the American Civil War] and never returned.[6]

REFERENCES

1. E Estyn Evans, *Ulster Journal of Archeology*, X, 1947.
2. Fynes Moryson, *An Itinerary*, IV, 1908.
3. MacLysaght, op. cit, 341-349.
4. *Béaloideas* 13, 1943, 130-57; 159-60; 161-72.
5. Ib., 4, 1934.
6. Op. cit.

11

Patterns and Fairs

Wild fruit was praised by poets from early days. Cherries, bilberries, whortleberries, apples, nuts—all were eaten and formed part of festive rites. A hermit who lived in the 9th century praised his hermitage which provided him with a clutch of eggs, honey, sweet apples, red cranberries, strawberries, raspberries, hazelnuts, a cup of hazel mead and good blackberries.

Blackberries and apples are referred to in glowing terms in the early lives and appear as desired objects in the Fionn tales. An entry in the *Annals*[1] under the date 1109 announces: "There is an abundance of apples this year in gardens and woods." According to legend St Patrick is credited with planting an apple tree on a certain occasion. Apples were listed in the foods allowed the Culdee monks: "In case of apples if they be large, five or six with bread will suffice for a meal, but if small, twelve apples are allowed." Again in a 12th-century poem we read, "I will eat good apples in the glen and fragrant berries of rowan tree."

The Anglo-Norman period saw the introduction of apple orchards in the south-east and this tradition of cultivation was reinforced by English settlers in the second half of the 17th century. South Armagh and the fringe counties of Down and Fermanagh were mentioned as places where apple orchards flourished. One of the loveliest legends of the apple tree remembered in Co Mayo tells of how the tree bent down to the Virgin Mary after St Joseph refused to pick the fruit for her. Ever since the apple tree in fruit is low with drooping branches.[2]

Dr Massari in his letters in the mid-17th century gives a full description not only of the fine meats, large oysters and fresh salmon which the ordinary people ate but such fruits as apples, pears, plums and cherries.

In wealthy households in cities and towns, imported fruits were often served as a first course: dried prunes, figs, dates, walnuts and almonds; apples and pears or plums were roasted and eaten with sugar at the end of the meal.

The more humble ate fruit when they could get it. Strawberries, cherries, apples and oranges were sold on the streets, even as they are today.

Patterns and fairs were a welcome break in the year at a time when people worked a six-day week and paid holidays were unknown. The pattern at Glendalough in Co Wicklow and Donnybrook Fair on the outskirts of Dublin were the biggest and best-known; ballads were sung about them, artists put them on canvas, clergymen thundered against them and the populace both wealthy and poor patronised them. They were colourful, rowdy gatherings where strolling players vied with itinerant musicians, and tinkers and trick-of-the-loop men sold their wares to, or pitted their wits against the wily and the innocent. Country fairs and patterns had their followings, and here too stalls piled high with silks and homespuns, pots and pans, gingerbread, cooked pigs' trotters and feet did a roaring trade. On 26 July 1829, Amhlaoibh Ó Súilleabháin described a pattern day at St James's Well, near Callan, Co Kilkenny, where there were "gooseberries, currants and cherries for children, gingerbread for young girls and maddening whiskey for those who wanted a row."[3]

In early Ireland and indeed until the late Middle Ages, vegetables were used mainly as salads or condiments or as pot herbs for cooking in stews and sauces. In the Ireland of the so-called Golden Age—the years between the coming of Christianity in the 5th century and the incursions of the Vikings in the 9th century—it was customary for hermits and anchorites to isolate themselves on some rocky fastness or in a remote glen and spend their days in prayer, often existing on wild fruit, fish and herbs. "Dry bread and watercress are pure foods for sages," observed one writer, and there is frequently mention in the early lives of cress and sorrel as part of the diet of holy men.

Herbs were grown in monastery gardens, and used for medicinal purposes as well as for flavouring food. In one of the law tracts we find the entry:

> No person on sick maintenance is entitled in Irish law to any condiment except garden herbs, for it is for that purpose, viz the care of the sick that gardens have been made... Every high Aire is entitled to have three condiments supplied for his nursing; honey, fresh garlic and an unlimited amount of celery.[4]

In time the monk's knowledge of gardening spread to the laity so that the use of herbs became widespread. We read in the *Laws*, "Every freeman is entitled to salt meat on his dish every 24 hours and from New Year's Eve to the first Sunday of Lent. On the other hand garden herbs are the condiment to which he is entitled in the Spring of Lent."

Leeks, onions and garlic added flavour to food; indeed the use of garlic was widespread, both as a flavouring and as a preservative. Nettles, which made an appearance almost six thousand years ago when the first farmers cut down forest trees to clear the ground for crop cultivation, were commonly used to make soup and pottage. They were also used as a vegetable in famine times. A story is told in the Lismore *Lives* of how St Colm Cille saw an old woman making a pottage of nettles for her supper and resolved that henceforth he would eat the same. "Pottage from this night onwards," he ordered his servant, "and bring no milk with it."

"It shall be done," said the servant, but fearing for his master's health he bored a hole in the stick with which he stirred the soup and poured meat juices through it into the pot, and so all unbeknownst nourished Colm Cille.[5]

"Shamrock" (in this context sorrel, not clover) was eaten as a salad, and also to assuage hunger in times of want. That inveterate 16th-century commentator Fynes Moryson caustically notes in his *Itinerary*: "The Irish willingly eat the herb shamrock…which as they run and are chased to and fro they snatch out of the ditches."[6] (He describes the Irish methods of war as skirmishes with retreats into forests and bogs.) John Dunton said, nearly a century later:

> They [the Irish] feed upon shamrock, watercress, roots
> [potatoes] and other herbs. Oatmeal and buttermilk they
> mix together. They drink whey, milk, beef, broth and eat
> meat without bread.[7]

Some varieties of parsnips and carrots were known in early Ireland. In the *Lives*[8] we read how St Ciarán of Saigher used parsnips as a relish, while Mac Conglinne in his 12th-century *Vision* gives a marvellous description of

> a row of fragrant apple trees, an orchard in its pink-tipped
> bloom between it and the hill, a forest tall of real leeks, of
> onions and carrots stood behind the house.[9]

While there is evidence that the Vikings of Dublin used some species of coarse black beans, peas and beans were not generally known or used in pre-Norman times. Possibly they were part of the new husbandry introduced by the monastic orders in the 12th century, and a little later they appear to have become well established as a food at least in that part of the country subject to Norman rule. While cabbage with potatoes and bacon or corned beef could be termed a national dish, the earlier wild cabbage was used mainly as a condiment or salad. The earliest reference to cultivated cabbage is given by a man called Stevens who encountered it in a garden in Co Limerick in 1690. Charlock or *praiseach bhuí*, an edible weed that when boiled resembled leafy brown kale was used from the 12th century and possibly much earlier. Mac Conglinne describes it as "the priest's fancy, juicy kale."[10] It was a famine food of the mid-19th century.

The asparagus was known as a table vegetable in the days of Dean Swift and is said to have been introduced from Holland by his patron, Sir William Temple. Swift described it as an excellent kidney stimulant and good for rheumatism and gout.

Pickled vegetables, walnuts and mushrooms were used in Britain from the 16th century onwards, and doubtless were known in the Pale of Dublin and in towns where the "New English" had put down roots and introduced new fashions in food. However, the ordinary country housewife used wild mushrooms freshly picked on a dewy morning from late June until mid-August, which was mushroom time. Early rising was said to be essential to harvest the best. Button mushrooms were delicious stewed in milk, with a good dab of butter and seasoned with pepper and salt. They could be thickened with flour or cornflour and used with potatoes or on toasted bread. When fully opened and just brown underneath they were known as platters and could be cooked on the gridiron, or fried with home-cured bacon. Mushroom ketchup was another "country farmhouse" favourite. Large fresh mushrooms were bruised, broken up, stalks and all, put into an earthenware jar or crock and covered with a layer of salt. Spices, saltpetre, cloves and red pepper were added. When the crock was filled and covered, the mushrooms were simmered gently for anything up to three or four hours and the contents strained through muslin and bottled. Or the mushrooms and salt could first be cooked and strained, then mace, nutmeg and black pepper added. They were then given a quick boil-up and bottled.

REFERENCES

1. The Four Masters, op. cit.
2. Department of Irish Folklore, MS ???, ??
3. de Bháldraithe, op.cit.
4. *Ériú*, XII, 1938, 25-27.
5. Whitley Stokes, (ed.), "Lives of the Saints" from *The Book of Lismore*, Oxford,1980.
6. Moryson, op. cit.
7. MacLysaght, op. cit.
8. Ib.
9. Meyer, op. cit.
10. Ib.

12

The Great Hunger

Tradition has it that Sir Walter Raleigh, favourite of Queen Elizabeth I, planted the first potato in Ireland in 1585. Certainly before the end of the century this new food crop had been introduced, a crop which, coupled with disastrous wars, plantations and changes in land ownership, was in time to gain such a hold that it completely changed the eating habits of the majority of the Irish. Traditional methods of brewing ale, of making cheese, of curing fish and meat, even in some places of baking bread were all but forgotten, and a country that had fed well on milk produce was now reduced to dependency on the potato.

The change in the food pattern was not sudden or dramatic. Food continued to be varied and cheap. There was a plentiful supply of fish and meat, while milk foods, porridge and bread were part of the everyday fare as they had been for a thousand years or more. Spanish wine, French claret, beer or ale and above all milk in all its forms were drunk and enjoyed. Various 17th-century writers remarked on how well the common people ate. Dr Massari noted that all victuals were sold cheaply, whether it be a large ox, a wether, a brace of capons, a hundred eggs or a huge loaf, and as for wild game, it was so abundant that people thought nothing of it. Still other observers described ships sailing from various ports laden with butter, cheese, tallow and salt. Butter and cheese were commonly sold at a penny a pound, likewise veal and mutton; a

large salmon might cost threepence, a hundred herrings the same.
"Pub grub", as it is known today, is not a 20th-century innovation.
For the modest expenditure of twopence on beer, the customer in
many a 17th and even 18th-century inn was offered as much bread,
meat, butter, cheese and fish as he could consume. Yet as the 17th
century drew to a close the potato was growing in importance
amongst the poor. Dunton wrote:

> Behind their cabins lies a garden, a piece of ground,
> sometimes half an acre, and in this you will find the turf
> stack, a few hundred sheaves of corn and peas. The rest of
> the ground is full of their dearly loved potatoes and a few
> cabbages.[1]

Almost a century later Arthur Young would echo these words
when he wrote that the food of the common Irish is potatoes and milk.

There were, to be sure, divergences in food patterns. In parts of
Ulster and Munster as much oaten bread and porridge as potatoes
was consumed. Certainly the potato had many advantages. Half an
acre was sufficient to grow a crop abundant enough to feed a family.
Potatoes were easy to cook, needing only a pot and a fire, and from
a nutritional point of view they provided a nearly perfect diet. The
average Irishman, who might eat up to 10 pounds of potatoes a day,
supplemented with a cup of milk with each meal and the occasional
helping of fish or eggs, was well nourished, with sufficient protein,
calcium, iron and calories for his needs. Kenneth Connell in his
study on the potato in Ireland says:

> For the lazy man there was no crop like it. It needed merely
> a few days' planting in the Spring, possibly earthing in the
> Summer, and a few days' digging in the Winter.[2]

Another couple of weeks might be expended on cutting and
gathering turf in the bog and for that expenditure of labour a family
would be fed and well warmed for the year. An additional
advantage was that pigs, cattle and fowl could be reared on

potatoes, fed on the tubers which were too small for everyday use.

People with a taste for travel could take to the roads soon after St Patrick's Day and settle down in the autumn to a leisurely life of small domestic chores, and the usual amusements of the time: storytelling, music and dancing to while away the long winter nights. The restless, ambitious man might spend his summer lifting the harvest on an English or Scottish farm, or hewing stones in an American quarry, for it was not unknown for men to emigrate to the New World for half the year and then make the long and arduous journey back home. The families of the absent worker often took to the roads to beg or seek seasonal work, but made sure to return home when the days began to shorten. Expectations were modest and most were content with a warm hearth and sufficient food to fill their stomachs. Parents divided and sub-divided their holdings to give a plot of land to the newly-wed son or daughter, who could live on little. Early marriages were common, the young were fertile, and children were welcomed, not only because they were loved but because they provided the only security that parents knew for old age.

In 1780 the population of Ireland was more than four million. Sixty years later, on the eve of the Great Famine, it had doubled to eight million, and some land holdings were so small that people could survive only if the crop was good. So long as there was sufficient to eat all was well, but for many it was living on the razor edge of want. George O'Brien, in his *Economic History of Ireland from the Union to the Famine*, writes:

> A population whose ordinary food is wheat and beef and whose ordinary drink is porter and ale can retrench in period of scarcity and resort to cheaper kinds of food such as barley, oats, rice and potatoes. But those who are habitually and entirely fed on potatoes live upon the extreme verge of human subsistence, and when they are deprived of their accustomed food there is nothing cheaper to which they can resort...there is nothing beyond but starvation and beggary.[3]

The potato disease which had manifested itself in North America in 1844 first appeared in these islands in the autumn of 1845 and made steady and terrible inroads. Apart from the potato, crops were good: wheat, turnips, carrots and green crops were plentiful and there was a good hay harvest. The blight appeared again in 1846, and was earlier and more widespread.

Father Mathew, the celebrated apostle of temperance, whose knowledge of Ireland was unmatched and who for a time almost wiped out the national vice of drunkenness, wrote to the Relief Commission:

> In the month of July, I travelled from Cork to Dublin and saw this doomed plant blooming in all the luxuriance of an abundant harvest. Returning in early August I beheld with sorrow one wide waste of putrefying vegetation. In many cases the wretched people were seated on the fences of their decaying gardens, wringing their hands and wailing bitterly at the destruction that had left them foodless.[4]

The famine was to drag on another year and the bitter wind of change swept millions away, either to paupers' graves or to the coffin ships bound for America and Canada. A Commissioner for Emigration in the United States wrote poignantly:

> If crosses and tombs could be erected on the water…the whole route of the emigrant vessels from Europe to America would long since have assumed the appearance of a crowded cemetery.[5]

Fast vanishing too was a way of life coloured by singing, dancing, and storytelling, and made warm by the age-old tradition of hospitality. Where once the stranger was welcome to a seat at the fire and a bite to eat, be that only a handful of roast potatoes, now every door was closed. Lurking behind every traveller and the starving beggar was the dread spectre of the famine fever with all its accompanying horrors. Down the centuries the Irish had been noted for their gaiety, their courage, their optimism and, above all, a love of their native place but the great hunger was to change all that. They fled in their hundreds of thousands, and for those who remained life would never be the same again.

Yet even after the famine years had passed, the potato continued to be a favourite food, easily grown and widely eaten. With all the variety of foodstuffs in our shops and markets today the potato is still a popular vegetable, nutritious, satisfying and not fattening, if like any other food it is eaten in moderation.

Traditionally the first crop of new potatoes was a cause for celebration. A special meal was prepared. A basket of potatoes was dug and the tender skins rubbed off. A three-legged pot was filled and the potatoes boiled on the open fire. When they were cooked the water was drained and the potatoes mashed with a pounder or beetle. Salt, pepper, hot milk, finely chopped onions, cooked green cabbage or kale were mixed in to make that most delicious of all traditional dishes, the much-loved colcannon, known in Donegal as *brúitín*.

REFERENCES

1. MacLysaght, op. cit.
2. Kenneth Connell, "The Potato in Ireland", *Ireland Past and Present* 23, 1962, 57-71.
3. George O'Brien, *Economic History of Ireland from the Union to the Famine*, London, 1921, 232-33.
4. Cecil Woodham-Smith, *The Great Hunger* London, 1962, 91.
5. Ib., 238.

13

The Red-Feathered Hen

Ireland long ago, heavily wooded, with lakes and rivers well
stocked with fish and mysterious mountains where the red deer
outpaced the wild boar, must have been a veritable paradise for
men whose delight it was to hunt and fish and who spent most of
their lives out of doors.

> Birds of the trackless woods would find their way into the
> cooking pots of the Fianna and the variegated nests from
> mountain pinnacles helped to light their fires.[1]

Exuberant birds and fowl are portrayed in the interlinear
drawings of that most magnificent of our illuminated manuscripts,
The Book of Kells; the purple eagle, the lordly peacock, the barnacle
goose, the domestic cock and hen intermingle and are interwoven
with fabled and winged animals and with the cats and mice,
beloved pets of the early monks.

Domestic fowl were bred from the early Christian era at least,
while birds called by name in the *Lives* are blackbird, wren, duck,
lark, swan, cuckoo, crane, raven, partridge, kite, hawk, sparrow,
eagle and stork. Giraldus Cambrensis, writing of Ireland in the 12th
century, mentions flocks of cranes, geese with prodigious croakings,
falcons, wild peacocks, wild hens, snipe, woodcock, pheasants and
nightingale as well as "clouds of larks singing the praises of God."[2]

Swans were served at great banquets in medieval times, though the flesh was said to be tough. Snipe, woodcock, pheasants, partridges and plover were caught and enjoyed. Large birds were roasted on the meat spit but while there were special spits for smaller birds, a traditional method of cooking birds and fowl was to roll them in clay and bake them in the hearth of a fire as if baking potatoes.

Four and twenty blackbirds baked in a pie was a dainty dish to set before the king, according to the nursery rhyme, and blackbird pie was served in Norman castles and great houses in medieval times, while blackbirds varied the diet of the common folk down to this century. In Inis Céin, Co Cork, in the 1940s an old man remembered how blackbirds and thrushes were used to supplement a diet of praties and salt herrings in hard times,[3] while in Rossport, Co Mayo, they ate puffins and other sea fowl which they found in openings high on the cliffs.

Robin Flower in his account of life on the Great Blasket[4] was told a story of how during the Great Famine when food was very scarce some fishermen returning home without any catch saw a great company of fine fat birds, puffins and guillemots, on a high cliff in Inishvicillane [Inis Mhic Aoibhleáin.] They would make good eating for the hungry islanders but the cliff seemed impossible to scale. Yet one of the fishermen attempted the climb while his companions closed their eyes in terror. He reached the mouth of the hole in the cliff, drove the birds in and throttled them, throwing down ten dozen birds so that they floated on the sea and were picked up by the curachs. They called to him to come down but there was no way he could and he bade them good-bye. "Home with you now in God's name," he said, "for I think these are the last birds I shall ever catch." But the story had a happy ending, for next morning at daybreak the fisherman's son rescued his father, and when once again he reached level ground so great was his welcome by the islanders that anyone would have thought he was Oisín returning from Tír na nÓg.

Geese were eaten from Michaelmas to Christmas and in almost every account of a traditional wedding in fact or fiction by an Irish author, the goose is sure to be served up. Carleton in his stories of pre-famine Ireland tells of a feast given by a wealthy farmer at which geese of all kinds, shoulder of mutton, laughing potatoes, carrots, parsnips, cabbage and an immense pudding were served.[5] Again in *Knocknagow*, Charles Kickham's story of life in Tipperary in the second half of the 19th century, we read how a plump goose, half boiled at Ned Brophy's wedding feast, caused much embarrassment before it was pushed aside and good roast beef and a companion goose (this one roasted to a turn) was served up. One of the guests attempted to cut the goose but to no avail. The story says:

> Now this young farmer partook of boiled goose in his own house on an average once a week—that is to say, every Sunday—since Michaelmas. But then the goose was always dismembered before it was put in the pot with the dumplings. And a very savoury dish, too, is goose and dumplings cooked in this way.[6]

While turkeys were known in Ireland since the 17th century, it is only in the present century that they are associated with the Christmas dinner. Possibly the goose was the first fowl domesticated in Europe. Certainly *foie gras* was a delicacy in 1st-century Rome, and the soles of goose feet which were grilled with cocks' combs were considered epicurean titbits for Roman nobles. Apple sauce or garlic sauce was served with roast goose stuffed with herbs and fruit in medieval times. Later, goose was stuffed with cooked mashed potatoes, breadcrumbs, bacon, onions and herbs. Geese are mentioned in the Brehon Laws, and a section dealing with poultry enumerates the fines for trespass of fowl and the measures that should be taken to ensure that poultry or cattle did not stray.

A yoke for pigs, a hood for hens, ties of earth for goats, a spancel for the yearly calves, a shepherd with the sheep and a herdsman with the cows. Hens found guilty of hedge crimes, that is of passing through hedges, had their wings clipped and a spancel put on them, and hens that were special pets paid an additional fine for trespassing.

Even the most faithful of pets have their faults, and a story is told in the *Lives*[7] of how a pet fox that belonged to St Moling fell from grace and stole and ate one of the hens belonging to the monastery. When the fox was scolded by his master he realised the enormity of what he had done and made his way to a nearby convent, where he stole a hen which belonged to the abbess. This hen he did not eat but carried back alive, though no doubt half dead with fright, to the monastery, where he laid it down at his master's feet, as if to say, "See how clever I am. I have replaced the hen of yours I ate."

St Moling hid his smile and chided his pet, saying: "You are an incorrigible thief; take the hen back to where it belongs and from this day on live without stealing, as other animals do." According to the legend the fox never again stole anything that belonged either to the monastery or the convent. What he did in the deep woods or on the mountain-tops we shall never know, for as the old Irish proverb says, "Nature breaks out through the eyes of the cat," and no doubt the same goes for the fox.

Roast duckling served with orange sauce is much enjoyed to this day, though in medieval times it was usual to boil a duck with turnips or with parsley and sweet herbs; or a sauce of clarified butter, seasoned with spices, accompanied the duck, which was served on wedges of toasted bread. In parts of Ireland it was traditional to cook duck with berries of juniper, known in Irish as *iúr creige*. Juniper berries, which were fresh-tasting were used for medicinal purposes and were also occasionally used as an ingredient in making *uisce beatha* or *aqua vitae*.

St Colmán's ducks were never in danger of being eaten. According to legend they were said to swim in a pool fed from his holy well near Templeshanbo in Co Wexford long after the saint's death. During Colmán's life, if any disrespect was offered either to the clergy or to the church, the ducks took umbrage and flew off to a distant lake and did not return until the sinner had done penance. Not only that, but for the duration of their self-imposed exile the waters of the duck pond grew muddy, unfit for the use of men or beast, and only regained their clarity when the ducks returned home. They were so tame that they took food from the hand and St Colmán decreed that they must never be harmed, let alone cooked and eaten. Once an ill-advised person stole one of the ducks and set it on a pot of water to boil. But no matter how hot the fire, the water in the pot remained cold and the little duck swam happily around until, in exasperation, the wrong-doer took the duck back to its pond. Even the animals were not safe from the saint's strictures. A kite which carried off a duck fell dead to the ground, while a fox that stole a duck choked while attempting to eat the bird. As was to be expected the duck flew back unharmed to the flock. The same legend is told of Innishmurray, in Sligo Bay, where St Colmán's ducks were said to live. Neither could they be cooked or harmed in any way.

Legends apart, fowl and eggs were important not only in the diet but in farmhouse economy. Women looked after the fowl and the profit made was theirs. It was usual up to this century for such produce as butter, fowl and eggs to be bartered for tea, sugar, dried fruit and small luxuries. Very often no money changed hands between a shopkeeper and a farmer's wife. Indeed hens were often the only source of income or pin money on which a wife could depend. Rearing fowl could be well worth a woman's while. Anne Slevin (née McGirr) from Eskragh, Co Tyrone, underlined this fact when in a recording made by her nephew Professor Séamas Ó Catháin of the Department of Irish Folklore, she remarked, "God be with the days when you could lift money off the street" (i.e. make money from hens). No feast, whether it was a wedding, the yearly "stations," a farewell to the emigrant or a welcome home to a son or daughter from across the ocean, was complete without the best of boiled hams, cooked fowl, great cuts of juicy beef, green cabbage, floury potatoes, and lashings of porter, whiskey and wine to wash it all down. Roast stuffed chicken and ham was the traditional Easter Sunday dinner. Amhlaoibh Ó Súilleabháin noted with great satisfaction in his diary on Easter Sunday, 6 April 1828:

> Easter Sunday and Christmas Day are the two best days
> for eating. Today I had chicken and smoked ham for my

dinner.[8]

Eggs were enjoyed as nutritious food from early on. Wild birds' eggs supplemented the diet for many people in spring and early summer when food was scarce and the crops had yet to ripen, and saved many a one from hunger in times of famine. The eggs of larger fowl were usually roasted but the eggs of smaller birds were often sucked out of the shells. A Roman gourmet named Apicius in the 1st century AD, wrote what was possibly the most famous cookery book for at least the next millennium. He made the use of eggs popular; his recipes included eggs boiled and served with sauces, or eggs fried in oil and served with a wine and herb dressing. Eggs were used for making custards and sweetmeats and to bind sausages and stuffings and as a thickening agent for a sauce.

Travellers and writers, monks who might spend time in the monasteries of Britain or France or some more distant part, brought back with them a knowledge of new and strange foods and drinks, like usquebaugh. Norsemen, Normans, Elizabethans, Cromwellians, Huguenots—the myriad settlers who made Ireland their home—introduced their favourite recipes and new methods of cooking which would be incorporated into the Irish diet. The monastery farm or the farm of substantial and wealthy folk no doubt produced quantities of eggs, but even humble folk could count on the occasional egg or two to vary the diet. Travellers bound for cities or sea ports, pilgrims en route to Lough Derg or Croagh Patrick or a holy well, would carry food in their bags like Chaucer's widow in the *Canterbury Tales* with her diet of milk, brown bread, smoked bacon and an egg or two.

Hard-cooked eggs with curds and cheese or apples were allowed to the Culdee monks at festival times such as Easter, and on other feasts they might have eggs and lard and the flesh of wild deer and wild hogs. Eggshells were used to measure liquids even as they are sometimes used in cooking today.

Hen eggs were preferred by women and children as sweeter than duck eggs, which were considered more substantial food for men and were greatly appreciated by turf-cutters or harvesters, who worked for hours in the open air and whose appetites were often great.

In early Ireland goose eggs were a luxury and at great banquets were served on dishes of silver and gold.

One of the most famous stories in the early literature is entitled, *The Banquet of Dún na nGedh and the Battle of Magh Rath*. It was recorded by Tiarnach, an annalist, under the year 637, and it is probable that the battle was an historical occurrence, though the supposed cause, the robbery of a basket of eggs, may be open to doubt. Be that as it may, by the 12th century, when the story was written down, goose eggs must have been so great a delicacy that it was thought they were worth going to war for. The goose eggs in question were specially requested by King Dónall, descendant of the legendary Niall of the Nine Hostages, and were needed for a banquet in his newly erected seven-rampart fort by the banks of the River Boyne.

The story goes that the king sent his servants to gather tribute for the feast, which would include the choicest of food; wine, venison, salmon, mead, metheglin and beer. Hardest to come by were goose eggs, but the king's men discovered a hidden hermitage in Co Meath where lived the holy hermit, Earc of Slane, whose habit it was to remain immersed in the River Boyne each day, up to his armpits in water and constantly engaged in prayer. Each evening he returned home, where he ate a modest meal of a goose egg and a half and three sprigs of the cresses of the Boyne. Despite the protestations of the hermit's housekeeper, the king's men carried away the store of eggs, and as was to be expected, when the hermit returned home that evening he placed a fearful curse on whoever would eat those eggs. Not even the prayers of twelve holy men, which included saints Colm Cille, Ciarán of Clonmacnoise, Mobhí, Ruán and Molaíse, could undo the harm. When the first goose egg served on a silver platter was set before the king's foster son Conghall, the platter turned to wood and the goose egg was changed into a hen egg. This was too great an insult to be borne by the men of Ulster and a fearsome battle was fought, though as the storyteller wryly concludes:

What is the difference at all between the egg of the red
feathered hen and the egg of the white winged goose. Alas
for him who destroyed all Erin for a dispute over an egg.[9]

REFERENCES

1. "Silva Gadelica" from Whitley Stokes, op. cit.
2. Giraldus Cambrensis. *Topography of Ireland*, trans. John J O'Meara, Dundalk, 1951, 19-27.
3. Dept of Irish Folklore. MS 462, 215.
4. Robin Flower, *The Western Island*, Oxford, 1944.
5. Carleton, op. cit.
6. Charles J Kickham, *Knocknagow or The Homes of Tipperary*, Dublin, 1887 (1949, 217).
7. Whitley Stokes, op. cit.
8. de Bhaldraithe, op. cit.
9. John O'Donovan (trans.), *The Banquet of Dún na nGedh*, Irish Archaeological Society, Dublin, 1842, 1-22.

14

The Year in Ireland

Festivals in Ireland were celebrated with a mixture of pagan superstition and Christian rites and beliefs: New Year's Eve and its charms and spells to keep hunger away for the coming twelve months; the first day of spring and the belief that St Brigid and her pet cow travelled the roads of Ireland and that crosses of straw should be hung in byre and stable and over the lintel of the door for luck; Shrove Tuesday and marriage incantations; Easter and the memory of the druid on the ramparts of Tara prophesying that if the Paschal Fire lit by St Patrick were not put out that night it would never be extinguished; May Day, the beginning of summer when magic was at its most potent and witches stole butter and cream; Midsummer's Eve, observed on the Eve of St John, 23 June—bonfires on the hills, young men leaping backwards over the flames to purify themselves for the marriage state, pregnant women stepping through the smouldering ashes to ensure a safe delivery of the child they carried; *Domhnach Chrom Dubh*—Crom Dubh's Sunday—the festival of the thunderous pagan god of the Celts, the older rites of hill-top climbing echoed in the bare-footed pilgrims climbing the summit of Croagh Patrick, the holy mountain, to hear first Mass at dawn; Hallow Eve, the eve of both the pagan festival of Samhain and the Christian feast of All Saints, spells and incantations to foresee what the future held in store; the great feast of Christmas celebrating the birth of the Babe at Bethlehem, in the shadows of the older Saturnalia, the pagan feast of the winter solstice. All of these festivals were occasions of mirth and merriment and the eating of festive foods and fruits of the season.

St Brigid's Day

The year in Ireland was traditionally held to commence on St Brigid's Day, 1 February. Some scholars have postulated the theory that in her persona we find both the Christian saint and the pagan goddess Brigid who was once widely worshipped, not alone in Ireland but amongst the Continental Celts. Yet as early as the 7th century three biographies had been written about her, based of course on tradition, but this is no reason to doubt their veracity. The *Lives* agree that she was the daughter of a slave girl and a wealthy chieftain and that she was fostered by a druid. She was beautiful, gifted and sufficiently strong-minded to oppose the powerful druid and her foster-brother when they attempted to marry her off to an eligible suitor. Instead she charted her own career, founding a monastery located in the Liffey plain, close to the hill fort of Allen. This in time became the principal foundation of the kingdom of Leinster, one part being reserved for monks, under the jurisdiction of an abbot-bishop, the other for nuns ruled over by the abbess, Brigid. It is said that Brigid in fact ruled the entire foundation, keeping the bishop for the purposes of ordination.

Both in the written sources and in folklore she comes across as a charismatic figure, warm-hearted, hospitable and as liberated as any woman who ever drew breath. She wielded immense authority, travelled widely, entertained with charm and grace and could be as moved by a starving animal as by a hungry beggarman. Like successful women everywhere, she was an excellent manager with a shrewd eye for a bargain and could outwit a mendacious king or chieftain. The 15th-century *Book of Leinster*, compiled from earlier manuscripts, is full of apocryphal stories of her sayings and doings, yet even here the sheer common sense and kindness of this remarkable woman shine through. Once, seven bishops with their retinue descended on her without warning. She had no food to offer them and sent her servant out fishing. He returned with a seal which she cooked so superbly and served so elegantly that they departed expressing themselves replete and happy. Another time she was cooking a side of bacon for equally distinguished visitors but was so moved by the cries of a starving dog that she fed him a large portion of the meat. Legend says that through a miracle the food multiplied but it is more likely that Brigid kept her guests so diverted with the tale of the dog that they failed to notice how scarce the rations were.

She was reputed to have been the best maker of ale and mead in Ireland and enjoyed her drink as well as the next. She was also said to have kept the best dairy. Her cows gave more milk than any other herd. The story is told that as a small child she could keep no food down, until fed on the milk of a white cow with red horns. It is traditional on St Brigid's Eve to leave outside every house a "strone" of oaten bread in the shape of a cross and a sheaf of straw on the window-sill for the saint and her pet white cow, who are said to travel the roads of Ireland on this night. It is also the custom to put out a length of cloth or ribbon known as *brat Bhride*—Brigid's mantle. Food and cloth touched by the saint are said to have curative powers.

Butter was always freshly churned on St Brigid's Day, and a cake, big as a cartwheel, baked, made of flour, curds, milk and egg. Mutton, bacon or a fowl, colcannon, boxty bread, dumplings and sowans were served at supper. A prosperous farmer might kill a sheep which he would share with neighbours and friends. After supper and thanksgiving rushes were made into Brigid's crosses and hung from the ceiling over the lintel of the door and in the dairy, where they would remain until the next St Brigid's Day came around. St Brigid could well be described as the patron saint of cooks and housewives everywhere.

SHROVE TUESDAY

This was a night of feasting before the black fast of Lent began. In order to ensure plenty during the year to come even the poorest made sure to have a little meat for their supper. For many centuries Catholics were bound by church law to abstain not only from meat but from eggs, milk, butter and cheese during the Lenten season. While these restrictions lessened as time went on, the three black days of fast, Ash Wednesday, Spy Wednesday and Good Friday continued to be so strictly observed that it was held that the child in the cradle should be allowed to cry three times before it was given milk.[1] Pancakes were always made on Shrove Tuesday night, called Pancake Night. The idea was that surplus butter, eggs, milk and cream should be used up before the Lenten fast began. The eldest unmarried daughter was allowed to toss the first pancake. Should the pancake fall to the floor she had no hope of marriage during the coming twelve months. Shrovetide weddings were popular in the not-too-distant past, a custom that sprang up when the Council of Trent in 1563 decreed that marriage could not be solemnised during the Lenten season.

ST PATRICK'S DAY

17 March was a welcome break from the Lenten austerities. Everyone should have meat for dinner on this day, both to honour the saint and as a relief from the Lenten abstinence. Amhlaoibh Ó Súilleabháin describes a meatless St Patrick's Day feast he shared with the local parish priest and some friends in 1829. They had fresh cod's head, salted marinated ling, smoked salmon, fresh trout with green cabbage and fragrant cheese, served with white wine, port, whiskey and punch in plenty.[2] Even men who had taken the pledge for Lent drank the *pota Phádraig* or Patrick's pot. A favourite couplet ran:

Good luck and long life to the Council of Trent
It took away meat but left us the drink.

GOOD FRIDAY

The week of Good Friday, known as Holy Week, was one of

extreme austerity. Bull's milk (juice of oatmeal husks) was used to colour tea which was taken with the dry bread for breakfast.

For dinner potatoes and salt were eaten, and for supper black tea, dry bread and occasionally porridge.[3] This diet was common over most of Ireland. Amhlaoibh Ó Súilleabháin describes how in the early 19th century, Kilkenny people fasted on barley bread, dry cress and water on Good Friday, a tradition that was remembered in living memory in the 1940s.[4] Even the dried fish or salted herrings which varied the meagre diet during the Lenten fast were not eaten during this period. However, gradually the penitential fare of earlier times was relaxed so that by the middle of the 19th century the "black fast" was observed on only two days. There were a couple of curious exceptions to the rule: certain wild animals and the barnacle goose were not considered flesh meat.

Tallaght, three miles from the centre of Dublin, was once the foundation of the Culdee monks. Their Abbot Maolruáin who died around 790 AD, laid down the rules to be observed by the community and these were inscribed on parchment by one of the brethren some forty or fifty years later.[5] Wild swine, deer or fowl were permitted as part of the food diet at Tallaght on festive and other occasions, because these were not considered flesh meat.

It was a common belief in medieval times that the barnacle goose (*Branta leucopsis*) did not constitute meat, and could therefore be taken during times of fasting and abstinence. Giraldus Cambrensis, in the 12th century believed that the barnacle goose was hatched from eggshells, while an English writer of the same period maintained that the barnacle goose had wings, feathers, neck and feet, laid eggs and tasted like wild duck yet was indeed a fish because it first grew out of a worm in the sea. Puffins were classified in the same manner and roasted puffins were part of the fish feast held for the enthronement of the Archbishop of Canterbury in March 1504.[6]

The folk belief that the barnacle goose was in fact a fish persisted in many parts of Ireland down to the present century. A certain hotel in Dingle was reputed to serve barnacle geese to the clergy for as long as abstinence on Fridays and certain days in Lent continued to be enforced as church law.

Eggs laid on Good Friday were marked with a cross to be eaten on Easter Sunday. Eggs set to hatch on this day were said to produce healthy birds. In medieval times all household bread baked on this day was marked with a cross, a custom that survives in the hot cross buns eaten on Good Friday. The tradition of marking home-made bread with a cross has persisted all over Ireland down to the present time.

For centuries people had abstained from meat for the six-and-a-half weeks of Lent, adding what little variety they could to their diet with dried ling and salted cod. Many existed on herrings and potatoes. It was usual to keep a barrel of herrings, salted or pickled, in the kitchen. A string of red herrings was hung from a hook on the hearth. Bacon, beef and salmon were cured or smoked in a similar manner. Apple wood was said to give a delicious flavour to smoked food.

Up to the beginning of the 20th century in places as far apart as Co Cork in the south and Co Monaghan in the north, butchers, who had sold little if any meat during the Lenten season, celebrated the coming of Easter by holding a mock funeral of a herring, or by whipping herrings through the streets of the town.

Henry Morris in *An Claidheamh Soluis* (1902) describes butchers walking in procession through the town of Dundalk, carrying a herring strung up on a pole which they beat to a pulp and hurled into the river. For the return journey they hung a dead lamb on the pole decorated with ribbons and flowers.

EASTER SUNDAY

This was the most important festival of the Christian year, a time for feasting after the lean weeks of Lent. Spring lamb, veal and chicken were part of the festive fare but the meal most enjoyed consisted of corned beef, cabbage and floury potatoes. When millions fled the country during and after the catastrophic years of the Great Famine they carried with them the memory of this festive dish, a tradition that survives in America to this day, though the meal is more often than not served on St Patrick's Day. As on other festive occasions it was customary for a farmer to share a bullock or lamb he had killed with his neighbours and less fortunate friends. It was traditional too that any beggar who called at the door would be given a gift of roasted potatoes. Eggs were in plentiful supply at Easter and were consumed in large quantities for breakfast, six per man being a moderate average. Eggs were boiled with traditional dyestuffs, herbs, plants and lichen to colour the shells for luck. Children made their own feast, collecting eggs and other good things from neighbours. They built a fire out of doors and roasted the eggs and potatoes, which they ate with bread and butter, sweet cakes, milk or home-made cordials. This custom was traditionally known as the *clúdóg*, a name given to the batch of eggs or to the little house or fireplace where the children held the feast. Still another Easter custom was to roll hard-boiled eggs down the nearest hill. Amhlaoibh Ó Súilleabháin notes in his diary on Easter Monday, 16 April 1827, that the day was commonly referred to as Easter Egg Day, and describes young men and girls eating their eggs and drinking in their local taverns.[7]

Eggshells, especially those which had been dyed, were kept to decorate the May bush.

MAY DAY

This was the time of year when magic was at its most potent and heralded the beginning of summer. The people of the *sí*, as the "good people" or fairy folk were known, were said to change their residence at this time, and woe betide the unwary traveller or young bride who might be swept away in the *sí gaoithe* or fairy wind. Spells were cast, witches assumed the shapes of hares, and milk and butter were vulnerable. Stories are told all over Ireland of a hare sighted milking the cows on May morning. When pursued by a hound or brought down by a gun the hare turns into an old woman with blood flowing from the wound.

Long ago people remained up all night on May Eve to protect their cows and it was the custom to drive the beasts between two fires on the mountain-tops to safeguard them against being "overlooked". Holy water or blessed ash was sprinkled on cows and also on boundary fences or tillage fields as a safeguard. Butter could not be stolen if a lump was placed on top of the gate pier of the farm, or thrown over the house or the dairy. In Garrycastle, Co Offaly, they tell how a certain man was passing a well one May morning when he saw an old woman skimming the well with a sieve, while she muttered, "Come all to me." He didn't believe in spells or the like and mockingly added, "and half to me." Much to his surprise at the next butter-making in his dairy he found he had half the butter of the townland.[8]

It was firmly held that most witches were out before dawn on May morn, gathering up the early morning dew with a cloth, a rope or a spancel, repeating the charm: "the tops of the grass and the roots of the corn. Give me the neighbours' milk, night, noon and morn." No fire was given out of the house on this day, and no beggar was welcome at the door. He or she might be a person of the Otherworld in disguise. In the manuscript material we find an account from Templemichael, Co Longford:

> They would not lend anything on May day for fear the luck
> would be taken away, nor would they like a red-haired
> person to cross the threshold.[9]

This has echoes of the age-old invocation made on Garland Sunday, when the first of the new potatoes were eaten and they said, "Death to the red-haired girl." Even the smoke rising from the chimney on May morn could be used to steal butter, by the simple expedients of walking backward and repeating the words, "the butter of that smoke upon my milk."

Likewise the good harvest which the diligent farmer might expect from his crops could be stolen away by some covetous person who had previously taken by stealth bread, meat or an egg from his neighbour's house and buried them with certain maledictions in a field. By this nefarious deed the evil-doer hoped that the farmer's crop would fail and that he or she would reap the rewards. To counteract this spell, it was necessary first of all to discover the buried food, which should then be burned. In its place a blessed candle, a rosary beads or some other religious object should be buried, holy water sprinkled and certain prayers recited.[10]

The first water taken from the top of the well by a milk skimmer after dawn on May morning was known as the luck of the well. Usually when milk was being dispensed on this day, a pinch of salt or a drop of holy water was added to prevent ill-luck. Some small token was expected in return: an egg or a coin. In *The Farm by Lough Gur* we have a colourful description of how the maids counteracted spells.

> They strewed primroses on the threshold of the front and back doors—no fairy can get over this defence—and in cow byres they hung branches of rowan, while the head dairy woman sprinkled holy water in mangers and stalls. The milkmaids at the end of the evening's milking, stood to make the sign of the cross with froth from the pails, signing themselves and making a cross in the air towards the cows.[11]

Housewives liked to have some special dish to celebrate the festival; a milk pudding, a cake, a curdy cheese or syllabub. Hall in *A Tour through Ireland* in the first part of the 19th century observed:

> On the first Sunday of May which at Cork and in most parts of Ireland is generally kept as Mayday; happening to be there on that day I found that all the low people, Protestant as well as Catholic, had gone out in the morning to get syllabubs or milk cooked in a certain way, and that many of them were drunk before breakfast.[12]

Earlier still Sir Henry Piers in his *Description of the County of Westmeath* in 1682 tells of a custom of making a type of thick milk pudding, rather like a blancmange, as a celebration and proof that the good housewife through careful management had sufficient flour to keep bread on the table during the winter months:

> They [the Irish] have a custom every Mayday which they
> count their first day of summer to have one formal dish,
> which some call stirabout or hasty pudding, that is of flour
> and milk boiled thick and this as an argument of the good
> wife's good housewifery that made her corn hold out so
> well, as to have such a dish to begin the summer fare with...
> even in the plentifullest and greatest houses where bread
> is in abundance all year long, they will not fail of this dish,
> nor yet even they that for a month before wanted bread.[13]

Eggshells hoarded from Easter Sunday, together with ribbons, bunches of flowers and coloured paper decorated the May bush which every family set up before their door. This custom has lasted down to the present time in parts of Meath and north Co Dublin. Closely associated with the May bush were the May bonfires which blazed not only in rural Ireland but in the Liberties of Dublin until well into the last century. Maypoles were set up in parts of Leinster and Ulster. Most famous of these were the two Dublin maypoles, erected at Harold's Cross and Finglas, described by Sir William Wilde (father of Oscar Wilde) in *Irish Popular Superstitions*.[14] He tells how all Dublin turned out to Finglas upon May Day to witness the sport and take part in the revels. This custom fell into disuse in the first half of the 19th century, but was revived in the Dublin of the 1920s and '30s, in pre-Social Welfare days, by Lady Aberdeen, patron of the Child Welfare Guilds or Baby Clubs. Meetings of these guilds for the care of children of the poor or working-class communities were held weekly all over Dublin. Once a year a fête was held in Lord Iveagh's gardens, St Stephen's Green, Dublin, where the various clubs competed for prizes. Children danced around gaily decorated maypoles and cups and medals were awarded to the most skilful team of dancers, the most colourful maypole, and the best guild. Bands played and tea, sandwiches, cakes, soft drinks, sweets and fruit were served to all in the best garden-party tradition.

ST JOHN'S EVE

The twenty-third of June was traditionally midsummer's day. Bonfires were lit on the hills and cattle driven through the *gríosach* or ashes, to prevent their being "overlooked". People brought food and drink to the bonfires; potatoes were roasted around the fire, and in the west of Ireland white bread soaked in hot milk and flavoured with sugar and spices was heated in a large pot and served to young people. Herbs gathered at this time of the year were said to be specially powerful. St John's wort (*Hypericum*) was known as the fairy herb because of its curative properties. When crushed it gave off an odour of incense, and was said to be a protection, and have special powers, against the evils of witchcraft. It was a well-known balm for the treatment of wounds and as a cure for rheumatism and bruises, and was a remedy for the "airy fit" (an attack of depression). A well-known green dyestuff also gathered at this time of year, foxglove (*Digitalis purpurea)* known in Irish as *méaracán na mban sí*—the banshees' thimble—was used as a cure for certain swellings. (The efficacy of digitalis in cardiac diseases is well attested.)

July was known as the "hungry month" in folklore. The harvest was not yet in and the poor subsisted on green cabbage, meal boiled with *praiseach bhuí*—charlock—and old potatoes, which were considered very inferior. However, as always, the more prosperous continued to eat very well. Amhlaoibh Ó Súilleabháin tells of being entertained to dinner by a certain Mr Power on 19 July 1827:

> Our host possesses a fine dwelling house, a substantial farm with a barn, a byre with 40 milch cows, splendid vegetable gardens, a herb garden and fruitful sheltered orchards. We dined on smoked bacon, white cabbage, magnificent potatoes and hot mixed punch and came home leisurely and cheerfully.[15]

Everyone looked forward to the harvest, and substantial farmers entertained their helpers and neighbours when the crops were in. This is a description of such a feast given in Co Clare in 1841:

A harvest dinner was given by a landlord to his tenantry.
We were passing along the tables, looking on at the happy
and hungry guests whose appetites had they been put up
at auction and offered for sale to a company of epicures
would have fetched extraordinary prices. Great was the
work of destruction going on upon huge mounds of beef,
joints of pork and mutton, pyramids of greens and potatoes,
enormous puddings, pies of Brobdingnag dimensions, jugs
of beer and jars of teetotal temperance cordial. One man
had a plate before him which was piled high with
contributions from every dish on the table, a large slice of
plum pudding resting very amicably beside a goodly
segment of corned beef, flanked with greens. Still he
seemed not quite satisfied—there was evidently something
wanting to complete his happiness. He had no potatoes.[16]

GARLAND SUNDAY

The feast of Lúnasa, celebrated by Irish country people on the last
Sunday of July or the first Sunday of August, marked the end of
summer and the beginning of autumn. Máire MacNeill treats of this
feast in an extensive and detailed study of the feast of Lúnasa and
describes how people climbed certain heights or gathered at water-
sides to spend the day in festivity, sports and bilberry-picking.[17]

The day was known by many names: Garlic Sunday, Fraughan
Sunday, Bilberry Sunday. In the broad sweep of country from north
Connacht across south Ulster and stretching into Tyrone and Down
we find the name *Domhnach Deireanach (an tSamhraidh)* — the last
Sunday of summer—and along the Irish-speaking western seaboard
and Corca Dhuibhne, the most portentous name of all, *Domhnach
Chrom Dubh*—Crom Dubh's Sunday. The name Lammas came in
with the English and Scottish settlers. It never passed into the Gaelic
sweep. Kuno Meyer writes:

Lammas Day makes known its dues

In each distant year,
Testing every famous fruit:
Food of herbs at *Lughnasa*.[18]

The name *Domhnach Chrom Dubh* has survived almost 2,000
years. *Crom Dubh*—the dark bent one—was a pagan god, dominant
in Ireland until the coming of St Patrick who, according to tradition,
overcame *"Cromh Dubh* and his sub-gods twelve." A legend, once
common, concerned St Colmán and the fruit picked on Garland
Sunday. When he left Ireland he first settled with his monks in the
ruins of a Roman fort at Annengray. Bilberries still line the path to
this one-time cave and holy well. Local tradition tells that when the
saint was weak after periods of fasting and penance he was
invariably restored to health by the bilberries.

This feast was once an important pagan festival, and the custom
of climbing the heights to pick fruit has survived down to our own
times. In some parts the outing has assumed the character of a
religious pilgrimage or pattern, the most famous of these being the
ascent of Croagh Patrick, the holy mountain, on the southern shore
of Clew Bay, Co Mayo, where, according to tradition, St Patrick
fasted forty days and nights.

Vivid descriptions are given in the manuscript material of the
Department of Irish Folklore of people dancing, singing, making
garlands, storytelling or gathering fraughans or bilberries at lakes,
holy wells, or more usually in the heights. Stalls were set up and
gingerbread, lemonade and fruit were sold. Often the festivities
were carried on into the night with singing and dancing in the
houses in the valleys below.

An account of such a gathering in Kilkenny, in a spot commanding
a pleasant view of the valleys of the Nore and the Barrow with the
backdrop of Brandon Hill and the Blackstairs Mountains, tells of
how young boys and girls for miles around climbed a wooded
height called Kylecorrage on the afternoon of Fraughan Sunday, as
it was locally known, to pick fraughans or bilberries. Back home
each girl baked a fraughan cake.

> This was a great honour conferred on the girls as each boy
> came to take the girl [to whom he had given his fraughans]
> as well as the cake to the Bonfire Dance that night.[19]

People feasted on beef, bacon, cabbage and potatoes, followed by blueberries, whortleberries or wild raspberries and strawberries with thick yellow cream. New potatoes were first dug for daily use in the week following Garland Sunday, but some were dug and eaten for the feast itself. It was not right to eat the potatoes without butter and when the first spoonful of champ (mashed potatoes mixed with onions, butter and cream, which was always eaten on Garland Sunday) was consumed, the age-old incantation was recited: "Death to the red-haired girl."

The essential significance of the survival of *Lúnasa* was that it marked the end of the period of waiting for the harvesting of the new crops and the first enjoyment of the new food.

MICHAELMAS

The feast of St Michael the Archangel falls on 29 September. In the old Irish tradition Michaelmas was known as *Fómhar na nGéanna*— the goose harvest. Geese hatched out in the spring were put out to pasture. These were known as "green" geese and were considered something of a delicacy. However, most geese were not killed until the grain was harvested and they were left to feed on the remaining grains. These were called "stubble" geese. A large grey goose with a tuft of feathers on its head like a little hat was known as an "embling" goose, or "rucklety" goose. In Co Longford, Michaelmas was remembered thus:

> Only an odd one kept turkeys in my young days, but
> everyone kept geese. People took the "grass of a goose" the
> same as they would the "grass of a cow". There would be
> ten or twelve geese in every flock. The geese were put to
> grass in May same as cows, and they'd sell around
> Hollantide when they'd take them off the grass.[20]

An old rhyme that goes back to the 17th century and was popular in the north of the country went:

> Geese in their prime season are
> If well roasted very good fare.
> Yet friends take heed
> How much you feed
> Lest your tongue runs loose:
> Your discourse shall smell of goose.

In parts of Ulster it was the custom to present the landlord with a couple of geese at Michaelmas, a custom that can be traced as far back as Edward IV's time. Michaelmas was the goose season and there was an old saying: "If you eat goose at Michaelmas you will never want all the year round."

Florence Irwin in her book *The Cookin' Woman: Irish Country Recipes from Ulster* gives a rhyme dated 1709 about some of the beliefs associated with eating geese.

> Question
> Yet my wife would persuade me (as I am a sinner)
> To have a fat goose on St Michael for dinner;
> And then all the year round, I pray you mind it,
> I shall not want money—oh grant I may find it!
> Now several there are that believe this is true.
> Yet the reason of this is desired from you.
> Answer
> We think you're so far from having more
> That the price of the goose you have less than before.
> The custom came up with the tenants presenting
> The landlords with geese, to incline their relenting
> On following payments.[21]

Everyone looked forward to the goose feast. In 1831 Amhlaoibh Ó Súilleabháin, the Kilkenny diarist, spent Michaelmas in Dublin alone but noted: "I had breakfast of beef and potatoes for 4d and

I ate some Michaelmas goose."[22]

According to country recipes the secret of a succulent goose was in the long, slow cooking. In the traditional farmhouse kitchen the goose was cooked in a "dutch", a heavy iron pot with a lid. The pot was placed on the open hearth and the lid was covered with sods of turf, which were replaced from time to time. The goose was stuffed with potatoes, onions, celery, butter, chopped lean bacon and seasoning. If a lighter stuffing was required, sage, onions and breadcrumbs bound with an egg were used. Boiled goose provided good goose broth, though it was said that a boiled goose was a spoiled goose. In the Glens of Antrim, and indeed in many other parts, the goose was parboiled to remove surplus grease. When the broth was sufficiently strong the goose was stuffed and roasted in a dutch or oval pot before an open fire.[23]

A traditional method of cooking goose comes from Blacklion, Co Cavan. The goose was covered in blue clay, that is blue marly clay, commonly called blue teel, or till, and then put in the heart of the fire to bake. When the time was judged right a piece of the clay was broken and a fork inserted to test if the bird was done.

> When the goose was taken out of the fire, the clay fell off and didn't leave a trace of feathers. Any bit of intestines, puddings, heart, etc. were dried up and you threw them away. There was nothing sweeter because everything was in it and nothing lost.[24]

This method was also used in the cooking of chicken and other fowl.

Goose feathers and down were used for filling mattresses and pillows. In many parts of the country the farmer roasted geese for the harvest feast for his workers, and the first of the corn was made into flour and baked into bread. The last sheaf of corn took pride of place on the supper table and the girl who had tied it was led by the farmer's son out on the floor in the first dance of the night. A favourite saying in the south and south-east of the country was "Lá Fhéile Mhichíl a chroitear an t-úllord"—On St Michael's Day the orchard is shaken—meaning the apples were picked.[25]

SAMHAIN

This ancient festival, the first day of winter, is traditionally kept on
1 November, which in the Christian calendar is the Feast of All
Saints. The vigil of the feast is Halloween, the night when charms
and incantations were powerful, when people looked into the
future, and when feasting and merriment were ordained. Up to
recent time this was a day of abstinence, when according to church
ruling no flesh meat was allowed. Colcannon, apple cake and barm
brack, as well as apples and nuts were part of the festive fare.
Colcannon was cooked in a skillet pot which had a large round
bottom, three little legs and two ear-like handles at the sides, and
consisted of potatoes mashed and mixed with chopped kale or
green cabbage and onions. Colcannon was so enjoyed it was
celebrated in verse:

> Did you ever eat colcannon
> When 'twas made with yellow cream
> And the kale and praties blended
> Like a picture in a dream?
> Did you ever scoop a hole on top
> To hold the melting lake
> Of the clover-flavoured butter
> Which your mother used to make?
> Ah God be with the happy days
> When troubles we had not
> And our mothers made colcannon
> In the little skillet pot.

Another favourite was champ, an Armagh name for a dish of
mashed potatoes, sweet milk, and chopped chives or onions, eaten
like colcannon by dipping each spoonful into the well of butter. It
was also the custom that when the first of the new potatoes were
dug they were made into champ. Boxty pancakes were another
Halloween favourite. Grated raw potatoes were squeezed in a cloth,
sieved, and mixed with baking powder and salt and a well-beaten
egg. Sufficient sweet milk was added to make a pancake batter.

These were served hot and well buttered and sprinkled with caster sugar.[26] They could also be made into scones called farls and baked on a griddle.

A favourite saying was :

> Boxty on the griddle, boxty on the pan;
> If you don't eat boxty, you'll never get your man.

and

> Two rounds of boxty baked on the pan:
> Each one came in got a farl in her han';
> Butter on one side, gravy on the other,
> Sure them that made boxty were better than me mother.

Apple potato cake or fadge was a popular dish in the north-east of the country, made with a potato cake mixture of freshly boiled potatoes, a little salt, melted butter and flour to bind. The mixture was divided into two, and rolled into rounds. Layers of sliced apples were laid on the base of the fadge; then the lid of pastry was placed on top. It was put down to cook in a pot-oven on a bed of red-hot turf. When the fadge was almost ready it was sliced round the sides, the top turned back and the apples liberally sprinkled with brown sugar and a good knob of butter. The fadge was then returned to the oven until the sugar and butter melted to form a sauce. A ring was inserted in the cake and it was believed that whoever got the ring would be married before the year was out.[27]

It was traditional that cattle should be taken in or housed in the byres and that all potatoes should be dug and all oats stacked by Halloween. Blackberries should not be picked or apples taken down from the tree because it was said the *púca* spat on them on the night after Samhain. In the Glens of Antrim they said that the devil shook his club at these fruits and shook his blanket at them.[28]

In north Leinster and parts of Ulster the old tradition of leaving food out for the fairies on Halloween was still observed in living memory.

A plate of champ, complete with spoon, was set at the foot of the nearest fairy thorn (hawthorn or whitethorn) or at the gate entrance to a field on both Halloween and All Souls' Night, 2 November. This was considered by some a ritual for the dead, by others an offering to the fairies.[29]

The association between food and the fairies is marked and this is especially true of the festivals, most of which had their origin in pre-Christian times. An informant in Layde, Co Antrim, describes how her grandmother used make thick oaten cakes with a hole in the centre on Halloween. A string was threaded through the hole and any child who came in had an oaten cake tied around her neck.

> The child could nibble the scone. It was also protection against the fairies. My grandmother used also rub salt and oaten meal on the crown of a child's head to keep it safe from the fairies. She always made apple tarts for this day.[30]

This ancient festival is still celebrated not only at home but in parts of Britain and all over the New England states of America. In town and country children still carry on the age-old custom of disguising themselves in masks and costumes and going from house to house collecting apples and nuts for the Halloween party. In America they say, "Trick or treat." After the traditional supper of colcannon young people played games involving ducking for apples in a barrel or basin of water, or allowing the peel of an apple to fall on the ground in the belief that it would show the initial letter of a sweetheart's name. A favourite pastime was for courting couples to sit around the fire telling stories and roasting nuts.

> When the nuts were really hot they were dropped into a bowl of water. A girl put her name on one nut, a boy on another. If the boy's nut spun away from the girl's nut it meant that they were not meant for each other.[31]

Almost all games and practices on this night had to do with love and courtship: the ring hidden in the colcannon or barm brack denoting marriage, or more disappointingly, the thimble foretelling spinsterhood. In many parts of the country the first and last spoonfuls of colcannon were put into the girl's stocking, which was then hung from a nail in the door in the belief that her future husband would be the first to enter. Still another custom was for a girl to go blindfolded into the night to pull a head of cabbage. The size and shape of the root denoted the size and shape of her future spouse: straight and sturdy or withered and crabbed. He would be rich if a generous amount of clay adhered to the roots, poor or mean if there was little clay. Finally the heart of the cabbage was a sure guide to his character. A sweet-tasting cabbage foretold a sweet-tempered man, while a hard, bitter cabbage indicated a sour-grained, cantankerous one.

Another custom was to cut nine stalks of yarrow with a black-handled knife. Part of the spell decreed that the girl must not speak from the moment she began to eat her colcannon until all the family had gone to bed. She then peeled the yarrow reciting the verse:

> Good night, good yarrow, thrice good night to thee!
> Tell me who my true love is to be.
> If his clothes I am to wear, if his children I'm to rear,
> Blithe and merry may he be with his face turned to me.
> If his clothes I'm not to wear, if his children not to rear,
> Sour and *gruama* may he be with back turned to me.

Still another charm was for a girl to eat an apple before a mirror at midnight while combing her hair. Her future husband would look over her right shoulder as the clock struck twelve.

The Halloween supper at home was always the most enjoyable feast of the year. On 31 October 1831, Amhlaoibh Ó Súilleabháin noted in his diary:

> A fine dry, cloudy day. I spent the night pleasantly eating apples, burning nuts, drinking tea and eating apple pie. This is how I ended the Autumn season.[32]

MARTINMAS

The feast of St Martin falls on 11 November. It was one of the few days of the year on which meat must be eaten, and traditionally a sheep or a lamb or more often a fowl—goose, duck, hen, or chicken—was sacrificed. It had to be be the best bird of the flock. This was done for protection. Those who had no fowl of their own bought a bird at the market for killing. In parts of the country it was customary for the better-off to make a gift of a fowl to a poor neighbour so that they could observe the Martinmas rite. Generally the woman of the house killed the bird at nightfall on St Martin's Eve. Blood was spilled on the door, on the doorpost, above the lintel or on the threshold, on the bedpost, over the fireplace and on the doors of the outhouse and cattle byres. Some was spilled on a cloth or piece of flax and kept for curative purposes. During the killing of the bird ritual prayers were recited: "I shed this blood in honour of God and St Martin to bring us safe from all illness and disease during the coming year." In Blacklion, Co Cavan, the head of the dead bird was thrown across the house three times for luck in honour of St Martin and St Brigid.[33] The bird was roasted and eaten by the family on the day of the feast. A bone of the animal or fowl sacrificed was kept to be cast into the midsummer bonfire on the feast of St John, 23 June.

According to legend St Martin was a miller who was ground in a mill-wheel. (Much the same story is told of the Norman saint, Thomas Becket, born in Cheapside, London, about 1118. However, unlike Martin, Thomas was supposed to have been saved by divine intervention.) Long ago it was customary to reckon the feast from Halloween:

Naoi n-oíche agus oíche gan áireamh
Ó Oíche Shamhna go hOíche 'le Mártain.

(Nine nights and a night without counting
From November night to St Martin's night.)

No wheel of any kind should be turned on Martinmas, be it mill-wheel, spinning-wheel or cartwheel—not even the heel of a stocking should be turned, which meant that no woman would knit on this day.

Fishermen believed that it was unlucky to take out boats on St Martin's Day. Legends are told of those who broke the taboo and saw omens and portents: a horseman riding towards them over the sea and in his wake a fierce and terrible storm; St Martin walking on water beside a boat—a sign that they should return to harbour before the storm broke.

Bad luck followed those who failed to fulfil the traditional custom of sacrificing an animal or bird. A farmer believes in the old ways but his son scoffs and refuses to sacrifice a bird. St Martin in the guise of a stranger comes to the house to tell the farmer that he will have his reward but that his son will suffer for his omission. Or a poor family, having no bird to sacrifice, kill their cat and as a result prosper during the year. When Martinmas comes around again they kill a cat though they can afford a fowl, and as a result of their miserliness they are dogged by bad luck and end up as poor as ever.

CHRISTMAS

In pre-Christian Ireland the winter solstice was a time of celebration when the dead returned. This belief of more than five thousand years can still be experienced when the sun illuminates the magnificent burial chamber at Newgrange on 21 December, awaiting the spirits of those long gone.

With the coming of Christianity in the 5th century the older pagan festival was replaced by the Christian feast. In the centuries since Patrick brought the Christian message, a host of customs and traditions, some with their roots in older times, have grown up.

Of all Christian festivals, Christmas was considered the most important in Ireland, and preparations began weeks in advance. Cattle and pigs were slaughtered and shared with neighbours. "Christmas boxes" of wine and fruit cake, tea and candles were given by shopkeepers to customers.

Candles were lighted and placed in the kitchen window on Christmas Eve to welcome the Holy Family, travelling the roads, seeking a place to rest their weary heads. It was a widespread belief that the ox and the ass knelt at midnight in honour of the Infant Birth, and that animals were given the power of speech.

The twelve days of Christmas, 25 December to 6 January (known as Little Christmas) were regarded as a holiday season, and the weather during those twelve days was taken as an omen for the coming twelve months. It was commonly held that during the twelve days of Christmas the gates of heaven were opened and anyone who died went straight to paradise. A fall of snow at Christmas was greeted rapturously, not only by children, who thought it a sign that geese were being plucked in Heaven, but by their elders, for in folk belief it indicated a mild spring. "A green Christmas makes a full churchyard," the old saying went.

Geese, ducks, great sides of beef, sheep and pork were turned on the roasting spit and the wassail cup circulated in the halls of princes and chieftains in early Christian and medieval times. In later times the Margadh Mór—Big Market—or, as it was sometimes called, the Live Market (because the fowl were still alive when sold) started off the season. In the not so long ago, country roads were alive with people going to the markets in the weeks before Christmas. Before dawn they rose to set off in pony carts, in horse-drawn carts or on foot, taking with them the turkeys, geese, hens, eggs, butter and vegetables they hoped to sell. Those who had no transport drove the flocks before them on the roads.

On the Monday before Christmas the second market or, as it was known, the Dead Market took place, when dead turkeys and geese were sold. With the money earned the women "brought home the Christmas": toys and sweets for the children, new clothes, tobacco, whiskey and wines, the best of tea, and the makings of the Christmas pudding—dried fruit, consisting of currants raisins, sultanas and candied peel; spice, sugar and treacle or golden syrup. All of these were used in the making, together with breadcrumbs, white flour, finely chopped suet, eggs and enough beer to wet the mixture. When the time came the pudding was mixed in a basin, then a large square of calico was dipped in boiling water, spread with lard or dripping and well sprinkled with flour. This formed a waterproof seal. The pudding mixture was placed in the centre of the cloth, the ends gathered up so that the mixture formed a ball and the loose ends tied with strong twine. It took ten hours to cook the pudding, which went down to boil in a big pot on the fire on Christmas Eve night. Many a housewife rose time and again from her bed to replenish the boiling water. "Cutlin" pudding was eaten in the days before the more palatable rich black Christmas pudding became popular. A thick porridge of wheaten meal was cooked, to which was added sugar, dried fruits and spices. This was wrapped in a ball and boiled in the same way as a Christmas pudding. The practice of the giving by grocers and publicans of a "Christmas box," consisting of an iced cake and a bottle of port or whiskey, to their customers continued up to the commencement of the Second World War in 1939.

Among the farming community it was traditional to kill and share out a beast at such festive times. John O'Dowd writing in *Béaloideas*, notes:

> I was informed by my father Patrick O'Dowd, who was born at Moorbrook House about two miles north of Foxford, Co Mayo in 1831, that it was the custom at his father's house to kill a beef at Christmas and Easter and that the local smith was entitled to the head.[34]

This custom of sharing is very old, and certain people were considered entitled to certain parts of the beast. The division was as follows:

> To the smith the head, tongue and feet; to the tailor the small ribs that go with the hindquarters; to the physician the kidneys; to the harper the udder; to the carpenter the liver; the marrowbone to the strong man; the heart to the cowherd; a choice piece to the midwife, another to the

stableman; black puddings and sausages to the ploughman
and sweetbreads for the mother; tallow for candles and
hide for wine and whiskey.[35]

Up to recent times many good Christian souls fasted and
abstained on St Stephen's Day, 26 December, to honour Stephen,
the first Christian martyr, and to ensure health for the coming
twelve months. Over the greater part of Ireland St Stephen's Day
is still remembered as the day for hunting the wren. Boys and girls
went from house to house carrying a holly bush on which a dead
wren was tied and singing the verse:

> The wren, the wren, the king of all birds,
> On St Stephen's Day he was caught in the furze.
> Although he is tiny his family is great;
> Put your hand in your pocket and give us a treat.
> On Christmas Day I turned the spit;
> I burned my finger, I feel it yet.
> So up with the kettle and down with the pan;
> Give us a penny to bury the wren.

NEW YEAR'S EVE

The last night of the old year was known in Irish as *Oíche na Coda
Móire*—the Night of the Big Portion—because of the belief that a
big supper on this night ensured full and plenty for the year to
come. No food should be taken out of the house on New Year's Eve.
On any other night of the year a hungry traveller or homeless waif
might expect hospitality as a matter of course, but on this night food
and drink were given grudgingly, if at all. It was better not to ask.
This custom went back to the time when the success or failure of
the crops meant all the difference between famine and plenty. Spells
and incantations were invoked to guard against the danger. It was
customary for the woman of the house in many parts of the country
to bake a large barm brack on New Year's Eve. As night approached
the man of the house took three bites out of the cake and dashed

it against the front door in the name of the Holy Trinity, expressing the pious hope that starvation might be banished from Ireland to the land of the Turks. The invocation went like this :

Fógraímíd an gorta
Amach go tír na dTurcach;
Ó 'nocht go bliain ó 'nocht
Agus 'nocht féin amach.

(We warn famine to retire
To the land of the Turks;
From tonight to this night twelve months
And from this night itself.)

A spell which was rather hard on the Turks! After the ceremony of banishment was over the fragments of the cake were gathered up and eaten by the family. In Imokilly, Co Cork, they had a custom that the crumbs were thrown at the door and windows to prove that no one inside was hungry.[36]

A rather more pleasing version of this custom from west Limerick is given by Kevin Danaher in *The Year in Ireland*.[37] The door was struck three times with a large cake while the head of the household recited:

An donas amach, a's an sonas isteach
Ó anocht to dtí bliain ó anocht
In ainm an Athar a's an Mhic a's an Spioraid Naoimh,
     Amen

(Happiness in and misfortune out
From tonight to this night twelve months
In the name of the Father and of the Son and of the Holy
     Spirit, Amen.)

Church bells ringing, hooters hooting, bonfires burning, people joining hands at midnight and singing "Auld Lang Syne"—these are now the customary ways to welcome the New Year; it is still considered good luck for a dark-haired man to be the first to cross the threshold just after the clock strikes twelve.

New Year's Day

New Year's Day was always known as *Lá na gCeapairí*—the Day of the Buttered Bread. This was possibly a talisman against hunger, or to show that food was plentiful. Sandwiches of bread and butter were placed outside the door on this morning. This tradition was described in an account from Luach, Doolin, Co Clare.

> Young people went from house to house early on New Year's morning, and it was customary to give them good slices of bread and butter and even poteen itself in the olden times. It wasn't seldom that poteen itself was in the story.[38]

The Twelfth Day of Christmas

The sixth of January, Little Christmas Day, or *Nollaig na mBan*—the Women's Christmas—was the day when all the dainties that women were said to enjoy were produced for high tea: thinly cut sandwiches, scones, gingerbread, apple cakes, sponge cakes decorated with swirls of icing, plum cake, brown bread, soda bread, baker's bread, pats of freshly made butter, bowls of cream, dishes of jams and preserves and the best-quality tea. Men had eaten their fill of meats and had often drunk to excess during the festive season, but this was the women's feast.

The twelfth day also celebrated the "Coming of the three Wise Kings" who followed their star from out the east, through desert and stony ways, clamouring cities, and low murmuring seashores. Did they pause by the waters of Babylon where once the children of Israel in their captivity remembered Zion? Did they stand for a little while on the mound turned to silver by the star, and faintly hear on the wind words that would one day echo around the world,

"Blessed are the peacemakers."? All we know is that they had no thought of turning back until they had found the Child and given their gifts. They are most joyously remembered in Irish tradition, as is the belief that in their honour, on this their night, the waters of the world are turned into wine.[39]

REFERENCES

1   Department of Irish Folklore, MS 485, 272-73.
2   de Bhaldraithe, op. cit.
3   Department of Irish Folklore. MS 1475, 485.
4   de Bhaldraithe, op. cit.
5   "Rules of Tallaght" (ed. E Gwynn), in *Hermathena* XLIV.
6   Anne Wilson, *Food and Drink in Britain*, London, 1962, 37.
7   de Bhaldraithe, op. cit.
8   Department of Irish Folklore. MS 1640, 115.
9   Ib, MS 1480, 68.
10. *Ulster Journal of Archeology*, 1855, 165.
11. Carbery, op. cit.
12. Rev James A Hall, *A Tour through Ireland*, London 1813.
13. Sir H Piers, *Description of the County of Westmeath*, 1682, 91.
14. Sir William Wilde, *Irish Popular Superstitions*, Dublin, 1853.
15. de Bhaldraithe, op. cit.
16. MDF. "Letters from the Coast of Clare", *Dublin University Magazine*. XVIII.
17. Máire MacNeill, *The Festival of Lughnasa*, Oxford, 1962.
18. Kuno Meyer (trans.), *Ancient Irish Poetry*, London, 1911.
19. Department of Irish Folklore, MS 890, 894.
20. Ib., MS 1408, 48.
21. Florence Irwin,*The Cookin' Woman*, Edinburgh, 1949.
22. de Bhaldraithe, op.cit.
23. Dept of Irish Folklore, MS 1360, 88.
24. Ib., MS 1804, 118.
25. *Béaloideas* XI, 1959.
26. Department of Irish Folklore, MS 2066, 99.
27. Ib., MS 1359, 138.

28. Ib., MS 7, 7.

29. Informant: Michael J Murphy, folklore collector.

30. Department of Irish Folklore. MS 1359, 140.

31. Ib., MS 1359, 138.

32. de Bhaldraithe, op. cit.

33. Department of Irish Folklore. MS 1839, 50.

34. *Béaloideas* X, 1940.

35. Ib.

36. "Traditions of Imokilly", *SOS. Cork Historical and Archaeological Society*, II, 1945.

37. Kevin Danaher, *The Year in Ireland*, Cork, 1972, 261.

38. Department of Irish Folklore, MS 39, 47

39. Ib., MS 1639, 330.

Some Traditional Recipes from Irish Hotels and Country Houses

COMPILED BY

KATHLEEN WATKINS

BALLYMALOE COUNTRY HOUSE AND BALLYMALOE COOKERY SCHOOL, CO CORK

Ballymaloe Country House, owned by Myrtle and Ivan Allen, and Ballymaloe Cookery School, owned by Darina and Timmy Allen, are not far from the fishing village of Ballycotton in County Cork. They are situated in the heart of the Irish countryside and the cookery school is now world-famous. There is something about Ballymaloe that is different from anywhere else in Ireland. The Allens are very professional people who work hard from dawn to dusk doing what they know best, which is growing good food, cooking it properly and serving it to people. What they all have in Ballymaloe is good food from the source, such as I have written about earlier. They have their own hens, their own farmland, their own animals, and all the fish comes from the sea in Ballycotton. Here are some of Darina Allen's favourite traditional recipes:

Spotted Dog

This is the traditional Irish "sweet cake," called Spotted Dog, Currie Cake, Spotted Dick or Railway Cake depending on the area.

  1 lb (450g/3¹/₄ cups) flour; we use all-purpose flour
  1 dessertspoon sugar
  1 level teaspoon (¹/₂ American teaspoon) salt
  1 level teaspoon (¹/₂ American teaspoon) breadsoda sieved
  3–4 ozs (85–110g) sultanas, raisins or currants
  12–15 fl ozs (350–425ml, 1¹/₂–2 scant cups approx.) sour milk or
    buttermilk
  1 egg (optional)

First fully preheat your oven to 230°C/450°F/Regulo 8.
Sieve the dry ingredients add the fruit and mix well. Make a well in the centre and pour most of the milk in at once. Using one hand, mix in the flour from the sides of the bowl, adding more milk if necessary. The dough should be softish, not too wet and sticky.

When it all comes together, turn it out onto a floured board, knead lightly for a few seconds, just enough to tidy it up. Pat the dough into a round about 1¹/₂ inches (4 cm) deep and cut a deep cross on it to let the fairies out! Let the cuts go over the sides of the bread to make sure of this.

Bake in a hot oven, 230°C/240°F/Regulo 8 for 15 minutes, then turn down the oven to 200°C/400°F/Regulo 6 for 30 minutes until the cake is cooked. If you are in doubt, tap the bottom; if it is cooked it will sound hollow.

Serve freshly baked, cut into thick slices smeared with butter.

Champ

This is one of the most delicious Irish potato recipes. A bowl of champ flecked with green scallions is "comfort" food at its best! Serves 4–6.

6–8 unpeeled "old" potatoes, e.g. Golden Wonders or Kerrs Pinks
4 ozs (110g/1cup) chopped scallions or spring onions (use the
    bulb and green stem) or 1¹/₂ ozs (45g/¹/₂ cup) chopped chives
12 fl ozs (350 ml/1¹/₂ cups) milk
2–4 ozs (55–110g/1–2 sticks) approx butter
Salt and freshly ground pepper

Scrub the potatoes and boil them in their jackets. Chop finely the scallions or spring onions or chives. Cover with cold milk and bring slowly to the boil. Simmer for about 3–4 minutes, turn off the heat and leave to infuse.

Peel and mash the freshly-boiled potatoes and, while hot, mix with the boiling milk and onions. Beat in the butter. Season to taste with salt and freshly ground pepper.

Serve in 1 large or 6 individual bowls with a knob of butter melting in the centre.

Champ may be put aside and reheated later in a moderate oven, 180°C/350°F/Regulo 4. Cover with tinfoil while it reheats so that it doesn't get a skin.

CASHEL HOUSE HOTEL, CASHEL, CONNEMARA, CO GALWAY

Many of our most successful establishments are family-owned and run and Cashel House Hotel is such a place. There you will find Dermot and Kay McEvilly. Dermot keeps a bit in the background and he works hard to keep the hotel up to the high standard to which it is run. Kay meets everybody in the evenings and at lunch and dinner. She takes the orders and hears where people have been during the day and suggests all the lovely places in Connemara and the surrounding countryside that they can go and visit. That is what our foreign visitors really love. General and Madame de Gaulle spent holidays in Cashel House some years ago and therefore many of the guests are French people.

The lovely thing about Cashel House Hotel is that Kay and Dermot's two sons have now qualified in the business. One has qualified at the International Training School in Switzerland and the other has qualified at Ballymaloe. They have horses and stables at the house. Their teenage daughter Lucy is a brilliant horsewoman and she spends a lot of time helping to run the stables during her school holidays. Cashel House Hotel is a beautiful place with a lovely atmosphere. It also has a beautiful garden. These are some of the McEvillys' most appreciated recipes.

Spring Nettle Soup

a bunch spring nettles
1 oz white flour
1 oz butter
$1^1/_2$ pints chicken stock
1 onion
$^1/_4$ pint fresh cream
salt and pepper
a pinch freshly grated nutmeg

Melt the butter in a pot. Wash and chop the nettles and the onion and saute with the lid on over low heat for 5–10 minutes. Add the flour and mix and then the chicken stock, bring to the boil and simmer for 15 minutes.

Liquidise, season with salt and pepper and grated nutmeg. Just before serving, mix in the cream.

Boxty

4 large potatoes
4 ozs butter
3 teaspoons salt
2 ozs white flour
chopped fresh herbs (optional): chives, parsley, thyme

Peel and grate the potatoes, put the mixture in a muslin bag or clean tea-towel and squeeze out the water and starch. Mix the potato in a bowl with the flour, add the salt and herbs.

Melt the butter in a pan, add the boxty mixture. Press down well and cook until golden brown underneath.

Turn over and cook for about 15–20 minutes. Cut in quarters. Serve with roast lamb or beef, or on its own.

Carrageen Mousse and Rum Sauce

4 ozs carrageen
1 measure rum
1 pint milk
2 ozs sugar
$^1/_2$ pint fresh cream
2 egg whites
lemon juice

Wash the carrageen and place in a pot with the milk. Bring to the boil and simmer for 10 minutes. Strain.

Whip the cream and fold into the carrageen. Add the sugar, rum and lemon juice.

Whisk the egg whites and fold into the mousse.

Pour into ramekin dishes or glasses and leave in the fridge to set for 2 hours.

Rum Sauce

$^1/_2$ pint cream
caster sugar
$^1/_2$ measure rum

Whip the cream, then add the sugar and rum.

MARLFIELD HOUSE HOTEL, GOREY, CO WEXFORD

Marlfield House Hotel is owned and run by Mary and Ray Bowe. It is a magnificent small country house to which they have added six new state-rooms. These are the most splendid hotel rooms in Ireland: for example the French suite has only the best French furniture, the Georgian suite Georgian furniture and so on. Their dining room is spectacular because they added a conservatory which really enhances the back of the house. Diners can look out over the lovely grounds as they eat.

This is a very upmarket establishment, beautifully run, and it is very popular with visitors to the Wexford Opera Festival.

Thin Slices of Salmon Baked with Sorrel Sauce

Serves 4

    8 thin slices salmon off the bone
    1 medium bunch sorrel leaves
    2 or 3 small fish bones
    1 glass white wine
    2 sticks celery
    1 onion
    1/2 leek
    4 peppercorns
    1 bay leaf; parsley stalks

Sorrel Sauce

First make fish stock. Sweat off chopped celery, leek and onion in a saucepan with bay leaf, parsley stalks and fish bones in some butter. Add peppercorns. Sweat without colour. Add one glass of white wine and reduce by half, then add one pint of cold water and bring stock to the boil.

To make the sorrel sauce: Reduce 3/4 of fish stock and 1/2 pint cream together. Simmer for 5 minutes until sufficiently thick to coat the back of a wooden spoon. Add the blended sorrel, bring to the boil and add seasoning.

(NB When the sorrel is added at the end of the recipe it stays a nice green colour and this is most important.)

Place the eight slices of salmon on a buttered roasting tray, season with a little salt, milled pepper and lemon juice. Brush the salmon with a little clarified butter. Cook in a preheated oven at 200 °C for 2-3 minutes.

Place the sorrel sauce on the base of the plate then place the slices of salmon on top.

Roast Stuffed Leg of Lamb with Caramel and Mint Sauce

1 small leg lamb with the aitchbone and knuckle removed
$^1/_2$ pan loaf white breadcrumbs
1 medium onion
Mixed herbs
2 oz butter
$^1/_2$ bag mixed nuts

Stuffing: Sweat off onions and fresh herbs in butter then add the breadcrumbs and season. Add chopped mixed nuts afterwards.

Make lamb stock by browning carrots, onion, celery, leeks and one clove garlic with the knuckle and the aitchbone. Add tomato puree and three pints cold water and bring to the boil. Skim when necessary. Cook for up to 1–2 hours, reducing liquid by half.

Caramel and mint sauce

Place 2oz granulated sugar in a saucepan and caramelise, then add reduced lamb stock and simmer for 10 minutes. Add the chopped mint and season to taste.

Place the stuffed leg of lamb in a roasting tin and season before cooking. Cook in a pre-heated oven for 50 min. to 1 hour at 225 °C.

Since the knuckle bone has been removed the lamb will cook more quickly. Pink lamb is much more flavoursome.

NEWBAY COUNTRY HOUSE, WEXFORD, CO WEXFORD

Newbay Country House is run and owned by Mientje and Paul Drum. Paul and Mientje used to live in Malahide and then they decided they would move and live down the country and it has been a very successful move for them. They are now living happily with their three children in Co Wexford. Paul trained as a chef in Switzerland, so dinner in the evening is a very special meal indeed, cooked by himself. Mientje is also a very good cook and she will often do the starter and the desserts. She is very keen on dried-flower arranging and she grows flowers for this purpose and arranges them in baskets and that is a little business for her. Paul is very much into pine which he gathers from around the country; he restores it and it can be seen on display in one of the rooms. The entire house, in fact, has bits of stripped pine throughout, and lovely curtains and bedspreads, all of which were made by Mientje because she is very talented with her hands. She is also a gilder, though she has not been doing any gilding recently, but she plans to get back to that work.

Newbay House caters not only for Irish but for foreign visitors, many of whom come in the autumn for the Wexford Opera Festival.

Hake in Wine and Tomato Sauce
Serves 6

Take six 4-oz fillets of skinned hake (or cod) and place them on an oven-proof dish. Cover with a glass of dry white wine and two glasses of fish stock. Season and place in a hot oven.

In the meantime, dice a medium onion and sweat in 3 oz butter. Add a few tablespoons of flour and cook for a minute. Into this mixture pour the juice and stock from the cooked fish. Add parsley and a tin of diced tomatoes.

Cook over a moderate heat, stirring constantly.

When cooked, add 4 tablespoons of cream.

Pour over fish and return to a moderate oven until ready to serve.

Newbay Brown Bread

1lb coarse wholemeal flour
$^1/_2$ lb pinhead oatmeal
$2^1/_2$ oz wheatgerm
$2^1/_2$ oz wheatbran
$2^1/_2$ oz plain white flour
$2^1/_2$ oz flake oatmeal
1 dessertspoon soft dark sugar
2 heaped and 1 flat teaspoon bread soda
1 litre carton buttermilk, at room temperature
Preheat a very hot oven, 450°F/230°C/Regulo 8.

Grease two 2-lb and one 1-lb loaf tins well and dust with wheatgerm.

Mix all the dry ingredients in a large bowl with your hands. Add the buttermilk (not too fresh—Min keeps it for a week or so) and mix thoroughly with a wooden spoon to make a wet dough. Turn into the prepared tins, sprinkle with wheatgerm, pat down and put into the preheated oven for 10 minutes.

Reduce the heat to 250°F, 130°C, Gas mark $^1/_2$, and leave until it has baked for a full hour.

When cooked, the loaves will sound hollow when tapped. Leave in the tins for 5 minutes to shrink, then they will come out easily.

Cool on a rack.

TEMPLE HOUSE, BALYMOTE, CO SLIGO

About fourteen miles from Sligo, on the Galway road, you will come upon Temple House which is owned by Sandy and Deb Percival. They farm 1,000 acres organically. It is a very special place and we tasted there some of their salads and a very simple rhubarb dish for dessert. None of us will ever forget the flavours. How I wish it were possible for us all to have more organic food. The Percivals have a great big mansion of a house and the table around which we sat to have our meal is in a dining-room which was last furnished in 1864. Temple House is well worth a visit. The Percivals have six double rooms which are not too expensive and you can have a meal in the evening that is out of this world.

Summer Pike

1 pike (about 3 lbs)

Clean the pike and leave whole. Take a fish kettle and enough water to cover the fish. Add 1 tablespoon salt and bring to the boil. Place fish in carefully and bring back to a simmer.
Cook gently for 20 minutes.
Remove and drain.
Place on an oval serving dish and surround with a variety of herbs—golden marjoram, lemon balm, variegated mint and green fennel.
Serve with minted new potatoes and a tossed green salad accompanied by a hollandaise and sorrel sauce.

Select Bibliography

Carbery, Mary. *The Farm by Lough Gur*. London, 1938.

Carleton, William. *Traits and Stories of the Irish Peasantry*. Dublin, 1830-33.

Connell, Kenneth. "The Potato in Ireland", *Ireland Past and Present*, 23, 1962.

Cullen, LM. *The Emergence of Modern Ireland*. New York, 1981.

Danaher, Kevin. *The Year in Ireland*. Cork.1972.

de Bhaldraithe, Tomás, *Cinnlae Amhlaoibh*. Baile Átha Cliath, 1970.

de Paor, Liam and Máire. *Early Christian Ireland*. London, 1958.

Derricke, John. *The Image of Ireland*. Edinburgh, 1833.

Dinley, Thomas. *Observations in a Tour through the Kingdom of Ireland in 1681*. Dublin, 1870.

Dunton, John. Letters, in Edward MacLysaght, *Irish Life in the 17th Century*. Dublin and Cork, 1939.

Edgeworth, Maria. *Castle Rackrent*. Oxford, 1969..

Evans, E Estyn. *Irish Folk Ways*. London, 1957.

Falkinder, L. *Illustrations of Irish History and Topography*. London, 1904.

Flower, Robin. *The Western Island*. Oxford, 1944.

Four Masters, The.*The Annals of the Kingdom of Ireland*. Ed. John O'Donovan. Dublin, 1845-51.

Giraldus Cambrensis. *Topography of Ireland*. Trans. John J O'Meara. Dundalk, 1951.

Hall, Mr. and Mrs CS. *Ireland, its Scenery and Character*. London, 1841-43.

Hall. Rev James A. *A Tour through Ireland*. London, 1813.

Herity, Michael, *Irish Passage Graves*. Dublin, 1974.

Hynes, Michael J. *The Mission of Rinuccini, 1645-1649*. Dublin, 1932.

Irwin, Florence. *The Cookin' Woman*. Edinburgh, 1949.

Kettle, Andrew J. *Material for Victory*. Dublin, 1958.

Kickham, Charles J. *Knocknagow, or The Homes of Tipperary*. Dublin, 1887.

Laverty, Maura. *Never No More*. London, 1942.

Lucas, AT. "Irish Food before the Potato", *Gwerin* III, 1960.

—"Cattle in Ancient and Medieval Irish Society." *O'Connell School Union Record*, 1937-58.

McGuffin, John. *In Praise of Poteen*. Belfast, 1978.

McGuire, EB. *Irish Whiskey*. Dublin, 1973.

MacLysaght, Edward. *Irish Life in the Seventeenth Century*. Dublin and Cork 1939.

MacNeill, Máire. *The Festival of Lughnasa*. Oxford, 1962.

Maxwell, Constantia. *Irish History from Contemporary Sources*. 1936.

—*The Stranger in Ireland*. London, 1954.

Meyer, Kuno (trans.). *Aisling Meic Conglinne*—The Vision of Mac Conglinne. London, 1892.

—(trans.). *Ancient Irish Poetry*. London, 1911.

Mitchell, Frank. *The Shell Guide to Reading the Irish Landscape*. Dublin, 1986.

O'Brien, George. *Economic History of Ireland in the 18th Century*. London, 1918.

—*Economic History of Ireland in the 17th Century*. London, 1919.

—*Economic History of Ireland from the Union to the Famine*. London, 1921.

O'Curry, Eugene. *Manners and Customs of the Ancient Irish*. I, II, III. Dublin and New York, 1873.

O'Donovan, John (trans.). "The Banquet of Dún na nGedh", *Irish Archaeological. Society* Dublin, 1842.

O'Dwyer, Peter. *Céilí Dé: Spiritual Reform in Ireland, 750-900*. Dublin, 1981.

Ó Súilleabháin, Seán. *A Handbook of Irish Folklore*. Dublin, 1942.

O'Sullivan, Dónal. *The Life, Times and Music of an Irish Harper*. London, 1955.

Rinuccini, Giocanni Battista. *Commentarius Rinuccinianus*. Ed. Stanislaus Kennedy.) Dublin, 1936.

Sayers, Peig. *Machnamh Sean-Mhná*—An Old Woman's Reflections. London, 1962.

Stokes, Whitley. "Lives of the Saints" from *The Book of Lismore*. Oxford, 1980.

—(ed. and trans.) *Tripartite Life of St Patrick*. London, 1887.

Synge, JM. *Riders to the Sea*. 1904.
—*The Aran Islands*. 1907.
Walker, Joseph C. *Memoir of the Armour and Weapons of the Irish*. Dublin, 1758.
Wakefield, Edward. *An Account of Ireland, Statistical and Political*. London, 1812.
Wilde, Sir William. *Irish Popular Superstitions*. Dublin, 1853.
Wilson, Anne C. *Food and Drink in Britain*. London, 1973.
Woodham-Smith, Cecil. *The Great Hunger*. London, 1962.

JOURNALS

Béaloideas
British Society of Franciscan Studies I. Aberdeen, 1908.
Rerum Brittanicarum II. Ed. JS. Bewer. London, 1862.
Ériú II, XIII.
"Rules of Tallaght." Ed. E Gwynn. *Hermathena* XLIV.
Indiana University Publications, Folklore Series IX. Indiana, 1957.
Ulster Journal of Archaeology, VI, 10, 1947.
Journal of Kildare Archaeological Society XV, 1971.
Journal of Clare Historical and Archaeological Society LIV, 1949.
Journal of Cork Historical and Archaeological Society II, 1945; LXXI, 1974.
Journal of the Old Athlone Society. I, 1972-73.

Index

The Homesick Garden

by
Kate Cruise O'Brien

"That's the trouble with trying to get your parents to like each other. They get sentimental instead. Or edgy. By edgy I mean they start edging the conversation towards sex, they start telling you things you don't really want to know. Mum made me feel awkward. I knew there was a time before I was born but I wasn't sure I wanted to hear about it—that way. In any case I didn't really see why she should feel so grateful to Dad just because he let her have a baby. I was the baby after all. I think he was lucky. But there was no arguing with Mum in this mood. She was wallowing in the past, getting to like Dad fifteen years too late."

The voice of Antonia, watchful young narrator of *The Homesick Garden*, the brilliant first novel of Kate Cruise O'Brien.

POOLBEG

Jimmy O'Dea

The Pride of the Coombe

by
Philip B Ryan

The definitive biography of Ireland's premier comic
actor, who died in 1965.

POOLBEG

Prisoners

The Civil War Letters of
Ernie O"Malley

edited by
Richard English and Cormac O'Malley

Ernie O'Malley (1897-1957) was one of the most
charismatic figures to emerge from the 1916-1923
revolution in Ireland. He was converted to Republicanism
during the 1916 Rising and remained an influential
member of the IRA during both the Anglo-Irish War and
the Civil War. *On Another Man's Wound* and *The Singing
FLame*, his autobiographical accounts of the period, are
classics.

These previously uncollected letters, written while Ernie
O'Malley was imprisoned in 1923 and 1924, illuminate
this important period in modern Irish history.

POOLBEG